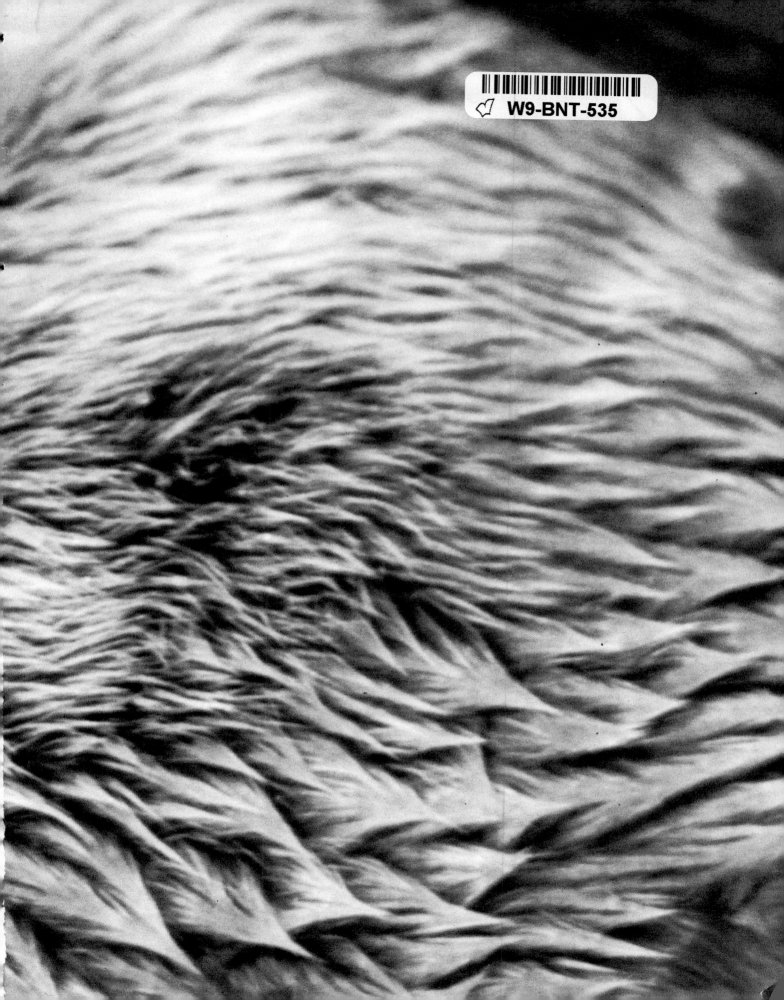

HARCOURT
Science

Harcourt School Publishers

Orlando • Boston • Dallas • Chicago • San Diego

www.harcourtschool.com

Sea otters are mammals. They live in the ocean near the west coast of North America. They can dive down 250 feet to find food. They roll on their backs and eat their food piece by piece. Otters spend almost one-half of every day licking themselves clean. The inside covers of this book show a closeup of otter fur.

Authors

Marjorie Slavick Frank
Former Adjunct Faculty Member
Hunter, Brooklyn, and
    Manhattan Colleges
New York, New York

Robert M. Jones
Professor of Education
University of Houston–
    Clear Lake
Houston, Texas

Gerald H. Krockover
*Professor of Earth and Atmospheric
    Science Education*
School Mathematics and
    Science Center
Purdue University
West Lafayette, Indiana

Mozell P. Lang
Science Education Consultant
Michigan Department
    of Education
Lansing, Michigan

Joyce C. McLeod
Visiting Professor
Rollins College
Winter Park, Florida

Carol J. Valenta
*Vice President—Education, Exhibits,
    and Programs*
St. Louis Science Center
St. Louis, Missouri

Barry A. Van Deman
*Program Director, Informal
    Science Education*
Arlington, Virginia

Printed in the United States of America

ISBN 0-15-322918-7

8 9 10 048 2006 2005

UNIT A
LIFE SCIENCE

Plants and Animals All Around

UNIT B LIFE SCIENCE

Living Together

UNIT C EARTH SCIENCE

About Our Earth

UNIT D EARTH SCIENCE

Weather, the Sky, and Seasons

★**7**

UNIT E

PHYSICAL SCIENCE

Matter and Energy

UNIT F PHYSICAL SCIENCE

Forces

★**9**

Investigating

This plan will help you work like a scientist.

STEP 1 — Observe and ask a question.

Which car will roll farther?

STEP 2 — Form a hypothesis.

The blue car will roll farther because it is heavier.

STEP 3 — Plan a fair test.

I'll start each car at the same spot.

STEP 4 — Do the test.

I'll measure how far each car rolls.

STEP 5 — Draw conclusions. Communicate results.

My hypothesis was correct. The red car did not roll as far as the blue car.

Investigate More

I wonder if the height of the ramp will make a difference.

Using Science Skills

Observe

Compare

Sequence

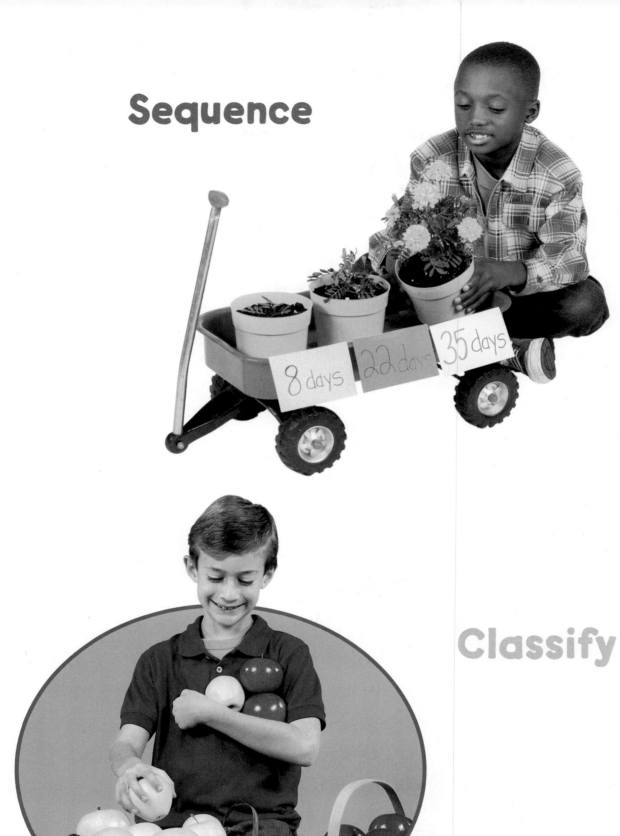

Classify

Infer

Form a Hypothesis

Make Models

Measure

Predict

Draw
Conclusions

How Many Paper Clips?

0 1 2 3 4

Communicate

Reading

A heading tells you what a section of a lesson is about.

A caption helps you understand what is in a picture.

A highlighted word helps you learn science vocabulary.

Ways Animals Begin Life

Rabbits are small when they are born. Their eyes are closed. They can not walk or hop until they are older.

just born   **8 days old**

■ **How do the chick and the rabbit change in different ways?**

Chicks **hatch**, or break out of eggs. Their eyes are open. Soon they can walk and peck for food.

just hatched   **8 days old**

A60

A picture helps you see what a lesson is about.

8 weeks old

adult

8 weeks old

adult

A61

A label tells you what is in a picture.

Some animals stay close to their young to keep them warm. Others keep their young warm in pouches.

Think About It

These questions help you make sure you understand the important ideas of a lesson.

Think About It

1. What are two ways that animals begin life?
2. How do all young animals change as they grow?

A63

Writing

Movement/Drama Link

Move Like a Frog

These children think about a time in a frog's life. Then they move to show what that time is like.

Write

Find an open space on the floor. Show what a frog does as an egg, a tadpole, or an adult frog. Then write about how frogs change.

A74

Write

Scientists write about what they learn. When you work like a scientist, you will do different kinds of writing. You will describe what you are learning and doing.

★21

Using Numbers

Scientists use numbers when they collect and show data.

Measuring

Scientists measure as they gather data. They use many different kinds of measuring tools.

For more information about measuring tools, see pages R2–R6.

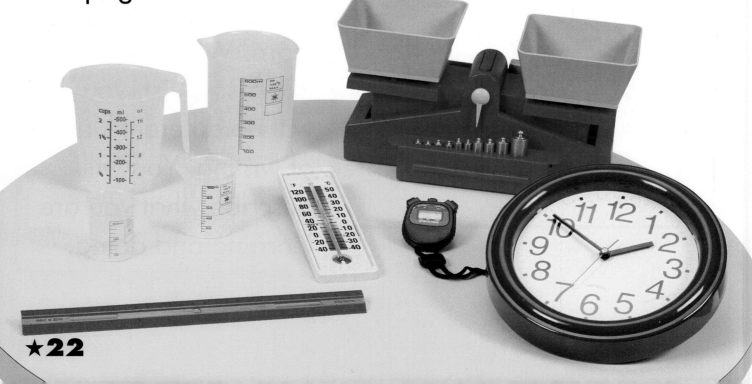

Interpreting Data

Scientists collect data. Tables, charts, and graphs are good ways to show data so the data can be interpreted by others.

You can read the data in tables, charts, and graphs.

How Much Rain?											
Winter											
Spring											
Summer											
Fall											

inches	0	1	2	3	4	5	6	7	8	9	10	11
centimeters			5		10		15		20		25	

You can also make your own tables, charts, and graphs.

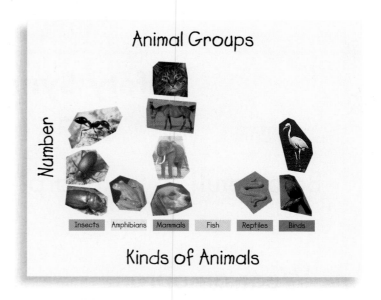

★23

Science Safety

Think ahead.

Be neat and clean.

Be careful.

Do not eat or drink things.

Safety Symbols

Be careful!

Sharp!

Be careful!

Wear an apron.

Wear goggles.

Plants and Animals All Around

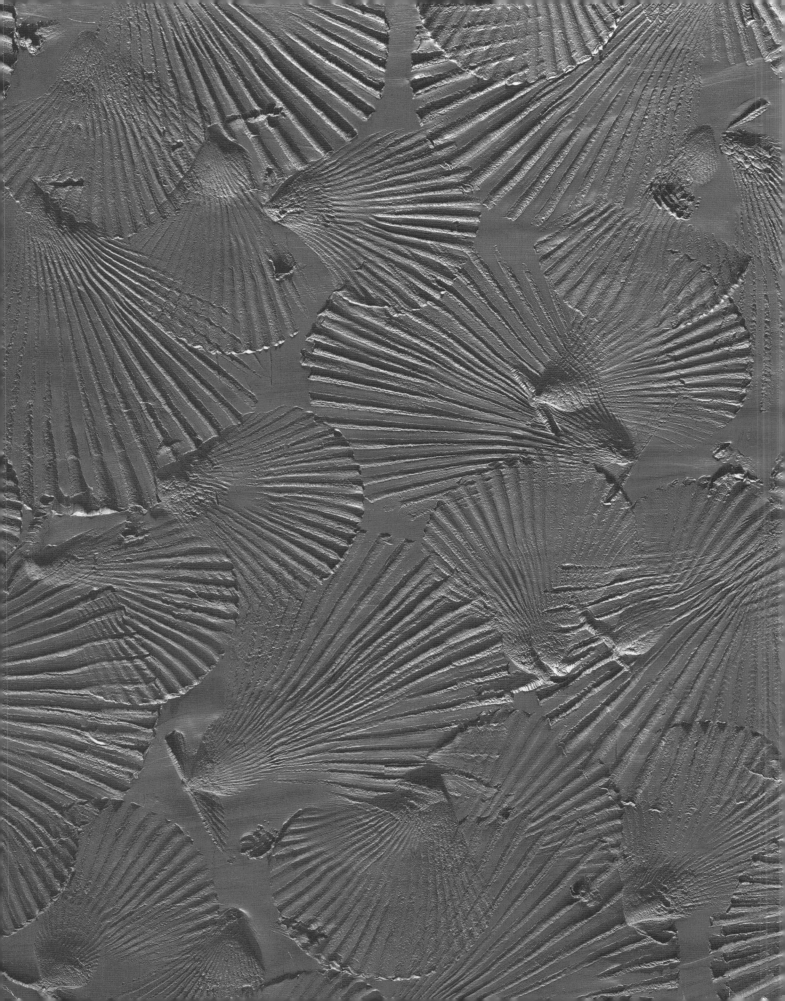

Plants and Animals All Around

UNIT EXPERIMENT

Seeds and Water

Do seeds need water to sprout?
Plan and do a test to find out.

Living and Nonliving Things

Vocabulary

senses

living

nonliving

Did You Know? Dogs have **senses** as people do, but dogs can hear sounds people can not hear.

A

How Do My Senses Help Me Learn?

Using Your Senses

You will need

pieces of fruit

plastic gloves

1 Close your eyes. Your partner will put on gloves and give you a piece of fruit.

2 Touch and smell the fruit. Tell what you observe. Name the fruit.

3 Take turns with your partner.

Science Skill

When you observe things, use more than your eyes to find out about them.

Your Five Senses

You have five **senses** that help you learn about things. What part of your body do you use for each sense?

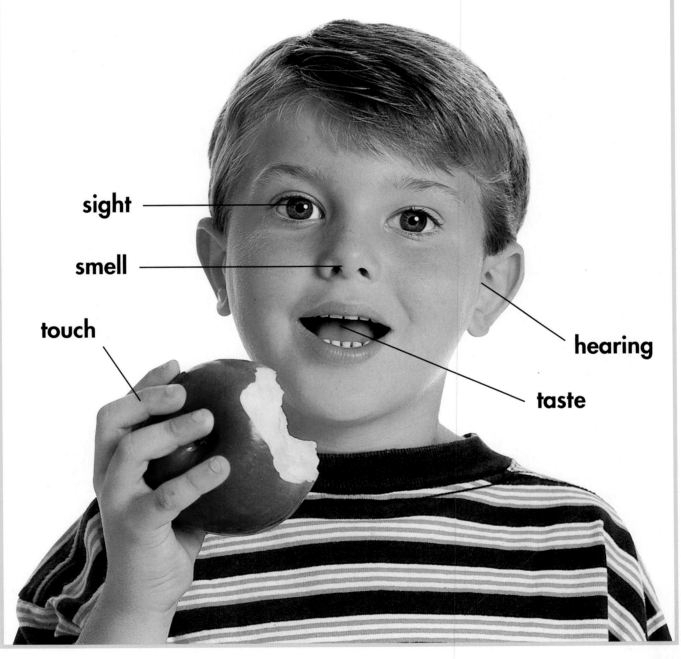

sight

smell

touch

hearing

taste

Sight

Your sense of sight helps you learn
how things look.

- **What can the boy learn
  by looking at the fish?**

Touch

Your sense of touch helps you learn how things feel.

■ **What can the girl learn by touching the kitten?**

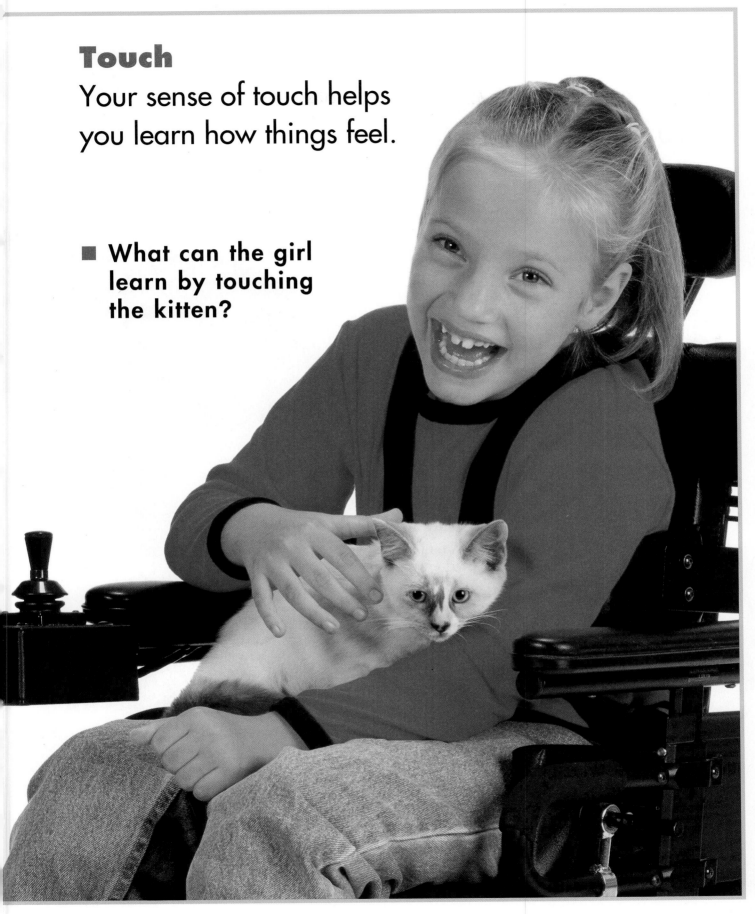

Hearing

Your sense of hearing helps you learn about sounds.

■ **What sound does this boy hear?**

Smell

Your sense of smell helps you learn how things smell.

■ **How do you think these flowers smell?**

Taste

Your sense of taste helps you know which foods you like.

■ **How do you think these grapes taste?**

Think About It

1. What are the five senses?
2. How do your senses help you learn?

What Are Living and Nonliving Things?

Investigate

A Mealworm and a Rock

You will need

mealworm

rock

hand lens

bran meal

1 Put bran meal near the mealworm and the rock. Use the hand lens to observe.

2 Does the mealworm or the rock move or eat? Draw what you see.

3 Compare the mealworm and the rock. Which is a living thing?

Science Skill
When you compare things, you tell how they are the same and different.

Learn About

Living and Nonliving Things

Plants, animals, and people are **living** things. They need food, water, and air to live and grow. **Nonliving** things do not need food, water, and air.

living

nonliving

Living Things

Flowers and dogs are living things. They need food, water, and air to grow and change. They come from other living things.

■ **How do you know the flower is a living thing?**

Nonliving Things

A rock and a chair are nonliving things.
They do not need food, water, and air.
They do not grow.

■ **How can you tell
these are nonliving
things?**

Compare Living and Nonliving Things

How can you tell if something is living?
Ask these questions.

- Does it need food, water, and air?
- Does it grow and change?

If you say yes both times, the thing is living.

■ How are these bears the same?

■ How are they different?

These pictures show living things and nonliving things. Water can move, but it is a nonliving thing. It does not need food and air.

■ **Which things in these pictures are living and nonliving?**

Think About It

1. What is a living thing?

2. What is a nonliving thing?

 Health/Career Link

A Doctor Observes People

This doctor is using her senses as she gives the boy a checkup. She listens to his heart. She looks at his throat.

 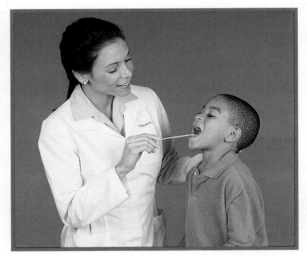

■ **Which sense is the doctor using in each picture?**

Write

Draw a picture of a doctor. Then show your picture. Write about how doctors use their senses in their work.

Math Link

Measure with a Growth Chart

This girl can tell she is growing. Her mother measures her on a growth chart. She is taller now than she was a year ago.

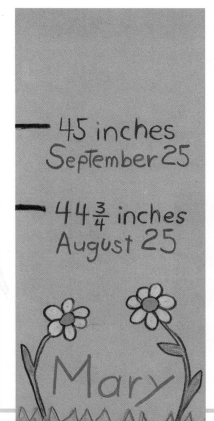

45 inches
September 25

44¾ inches
August 25

Mary

Think and Do

Make a growth chart. Have someone help you mark how tall you are. Write the date. Measure and write how tall you are each month.

Tell What You Know

1. Which senses would you use to learn more about each thing?

Vocabulary

Tell which pictures go with the words.

2. living thing

3. nonliving thing

a.   **b.**   **c.**   **d.**

Using Science Skills

4. **Observe** Collect things in an egg carton. Use two words to tell how each thing feels, looks, sounds, or smells. Have a partner guess each thing.

5. **Compare** Make a chart to compare a pencil and a plant. Draw pictures of them. Tell if the things are living or nonliving.

Living or Nonliving?			
Thing	Picture	Does it need air and water?	Does it grow?
pencil			
plant			

CHAPTER 2

All About Plants

Vocabulary

roots
stem
leaves
flowers
seed
seed coat
sunlight

Did You Know?
The rafflesia is the biggest **flower** in the world.

Did You Know?
There is a plant that has **leaves** that look like elephant ears.

What Are the Parts of a Plant?

Plant Parts

You will need

carrot

plant with flower

paper and pencil

1 Look at the parts of one plant. Draw what you see.

2 Look at the parts of the other plant. Draw what you see.

3 Compare the plants. Tell about their parts.

Science Skill

When you compare things, you tell how they are the same and different.

Parts of a Plant

Plants have different parts. Most plants have roots, a stem, and leaves. Many plants also have flowers.

flower

leaf

stem

roots

How Plant Parts Help a Plant

Plants have many shapes and sizes.
Most plants have the same parts.
These parts help them live and grow.

Roots

The **roots** hold
plants in the soil. The
roots also take in water.

■ **What part of a carrot
do you eat?**

■ **Where are the stems in these pictures?**

Stems

The **stem** helps hold up the plant. Water moves up the stem to the leaves.

A tree trunk is also a stem. Water moves up the trunk to the tree's leaves.

Leaves

The **leaves** make food for the plant. Leaves from different plants have different shapes.

■ **What shapes do you see?**

Flowers

Many plants also have flowers.
The **flowers** make seeds.

■ **What part of the plant is this bee on?**

Think About It

1. How are plants the same?

2. How are they different?

How Do Plants Grow?

 Investigate

The Inside of a Seed

You will need

bean seed

hand lens

1 Peel off the covering of the seed.

2 Open the seed.

3 Observe. Tell what is inside.

Science Skill
Use a hand lens to help you observe.

How Plants Grow

Most plants grow from a **seed**. The seed may have a covering called a **seed coat**. The seed coat falls away as the plant grows.

leaves

stem

seed

seed coat

roots

Plants Grow from Seeds

Different plants grow from different seeds. The new plants look like the plants the seeds came from. When old plants die, their seeds can be planted to grow new plants.

■ **Observe the seeds. How are they the same and different?**

tomato seeds

sunflower seeds

apple seeds

corn seeds

dandelion seeds

orange seeds

Think About It

1. Where do new plants come from?

2. What will the plant that grows from a seed look like?

What Do Plants Need?

What Plants Need to Grow

You will need

seeds

2 clear cups

any color cup

soil

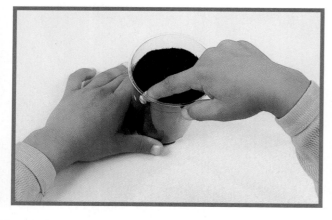

1 Fill one clear cup with soil. Plant two seeds near the side. Water.

2 Put the cup with the seeds into the cup with color. After 3 days, take it out.

3 Share what you see.

Science Skill

When you share your ideas, you **communicate** with others.

What Plants Need to Live

Plants need four things to live and grow.
What are these four things?

air

light

soil

water

How Plants Grow and Live

Light and Air

A plant's leaves use light and air to make the plant's food. Light from the sun is called **sunlight**.

Water

Plants also need water to grow and stay healthy. Water helps move food to all parts of the plant.

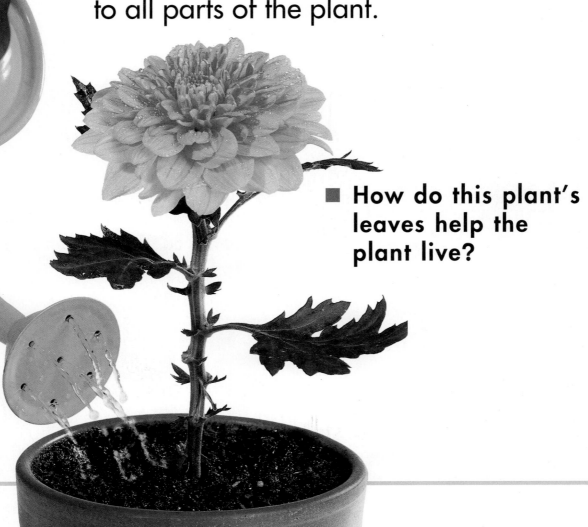

■ How do this plant's leaves help the plant live?

A Place to Grow

Different kinds of plants grow in different places around the world. All these plants need light, air, and water.

■ **Where is the water in each of these pictures?**

Think About It

1. What do plants need to live and grow?

2. How do leaves use light and air?

 Art Link

An Artist Observes Plants

An artist named Vincent van Gogh painted these flowers long ago. Artists look closely at things around them.

■ **What parts of a plant can you see in this picture?**

■ **What part is missing?**

Sunflowers **by Vincent van Gogh**

flower

stem

This plant has a flower.
Water moves up the stem.

Write

Paint your own picture of a plant. Label and write about two parts.

Math Link

Measure a Plant

You can use a ruler to measure how tall a plant grows. You can also use a pencil or a stick if you do not have a ruler.

Think and Do

Watch a plant grow. Put a pencil in the soil next to the plant. Mark how tall the plant is. Every three days, mark how much the plant has grown.

Tell What You Know

1. Tell what you know about each picture.

Vocabulary

Tell which picture goes with each word or words.

2. roots

3. leaves

4. stem

5. flowers

6. sunlight

7. seed

8. seed coat

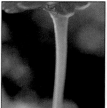
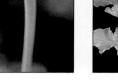

a. **b.** **c.** **d.**

e. **f.** **g.**

Using Science Skills

9. **Compare** Roots take in water. Stems help plants stand up. Think about the parts of your body that take in water or help you stand up. How are you the same as a plant? How are you different?

10. **Observe** Make a chart about leaves where you live.

Find two leaves. Glue or tape them on your chart. Tell about your leaves.

Leaves			
Leaf	Shape	Color	Size

CHAPTER 3

All About Animals

Vocabulary

gills
mammal
reptile
amphibian
insect
hatch
larva
pupa
tadpoles

Did You Know?
A gecko is a **reptile** that can crawl up trees.

Did You Know?
There are more kinds of beetles than any other kind of **insect**.

What Do Animals Need?

 Investigate

An Animal Home

You will need

plastic box
and gloves

soil, twig,
and rocks

water in a
bottle cap

small
animals

1 Put the soil, twig, rocks, water, and animals in the box.

2 Observe. How does your home give the animals food, water, and a place to hide?

3 Draw what you see. Close the lid.

Science Skill
When you observe the animals in their home, you can see how they meet their needs.

What Animals Need

All animals need food, water, air, and a place to live. These ducks live by a pond. Why is this a good home for them?

mallard ducks

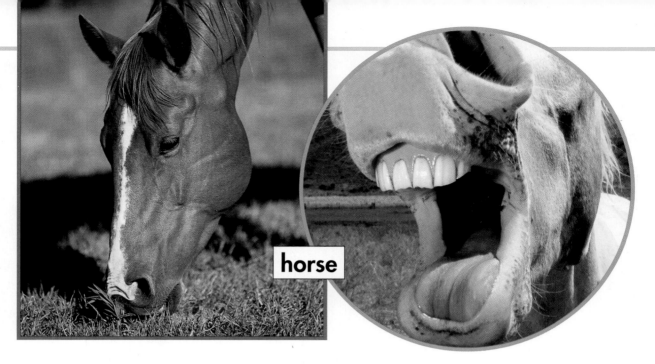

horse

Animals Need Food

Different kinds of animals need different kinds of food to live and grow. Horses eat grass, but lions eat meat. A horse's flat teeth are good for chewing grass. A lion's sharp teeth are good for tearing meat.

mountain lion

■ **What do an animal's teeth tell you about what it eats?**

Animals Need Water

All animals need water to live. Like many animals, a camel drinks with its mouth. It also gets water from the food it eats. An elephant uses its trunk to put water in its mouth.

■ **How are the camels and the elephant getting the water they need?**

camels

elephant

Animals Need a Place to Live

All animals need a place to live. A bat can find a home in a cave. A falcon can build a nest. Animals keep safe and raise their young in their homes.

bat

peregrine falcons

Park Ranger

Many animals have homes in parks. If they need help, park rangers take care of them.

Animals Need Air

All animals need air to live and grow. Special body parts help them get it. Some animals have a nose and lungs. Others, like this fish, have **gills** that take air from water.

COW

gill covering

Think About It

1. What do animals need to live and grow?
2. What are some ways animals meet these needs?

What Are Some Kinds of Animals?

Investigate

Animals in Your Neighborhood

You will need

paper and pencil

1 Observe different kinds of animals in your schoolyard.

2 Draw a picture of each animal you observe.

3 Classify the animals into groups. How are the animals in each group the same?

Science Skill
When you classify animals, you observe how they are the same. Then you group them.

Different Kinds of Animals

reptile

Scientists observe how animals are the same and different. They put animals that are the same into groups. Here are some kinds of animals.

birds

mammal

fish

amphibian

A49

Mammals

A **mammal** is an animal that feeds milk to its young. A mammal also has hair or fur on its body.

■ How can you tell these animals are mammals?

whitetail deer

pig

squirrel

Birds

Birds are animals that have two wings and two feet. They are the only animals that have feathers. Some birds fly, some birds run, and some swim.

macaw

bluebird

flamingo

■ **How are all these birds the same?**

Reptiles

A **reptile** is an animal with rough, dry skin. It may have scales or hard plates. Alligators and turtles are reptiles.

alligators

giant tortoise

Amphibians

An **amphibian** is an animal with smooth, wet skin. Frogs, toads, and salamanders are amphibians.

salamander

■ How are amphibians different from reptiles?

Fish

Fish live in water. They have special body parts called gills that help them breathe. Their bodies are covered with scales.

snapper

gill covering

queen angelfish

■ **How are these fish the same?**

Think About It

1. What are some different kinds of animals?
2. How are the animals in all the groups the same? How are they different?

What Are Insects?

Investigate

A Model of an Insect

You will need

Styrofoam balls

scissors

toothpicks and chenille sticks

wax paper

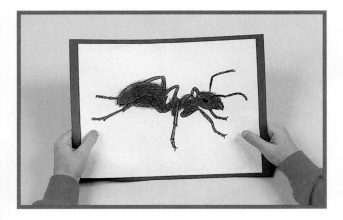

1 Choose an insect to make. Insects have three body parts and six legs.

2 Choose materials. Make a model of your insect.

 CAUTION Be careful with toothpicks, chenille sticks, and scissors. They are sharp.

3 Compare your model with a picture of a real insect.

Science Skill

When you make a model of an insect, you show parts that a real insect has.

Insects

An **insect** is an animal that has three body parts and six legs. Some insects also have wings.

3 body parts

weevil

More About Insects

Insects lay eggs. A ladybug lays hundreds of eggs at one time.

Insects do not have bones. They have a strong body covering. The covering keeps their soft insides safe.

ladybug

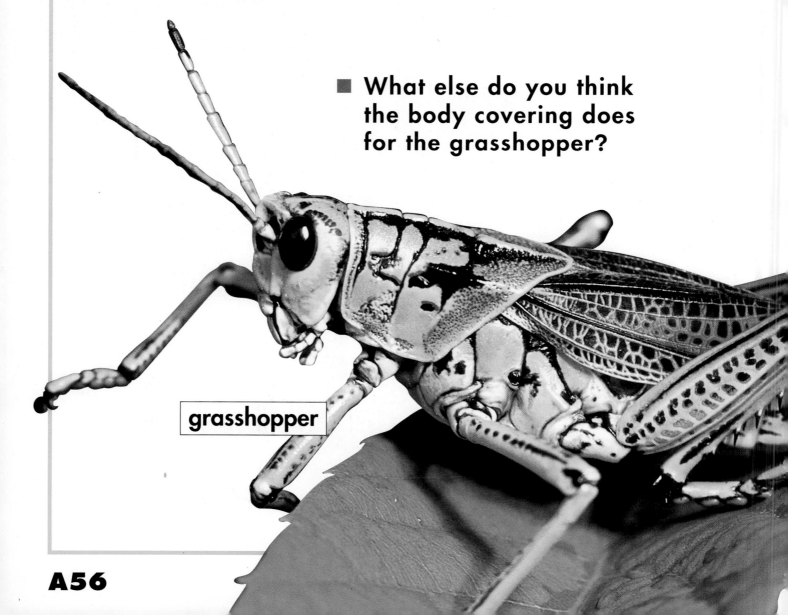

■ **What else do you think the body covering does for the grasshopper?**

grasshopper

A butterfly is an insect. It uses its wings to fly. An ant is an insect, too. Most ants have no wings. They use their legs to move.

■ **How are the butterfly and the ant the same and different?**

butterfly

ant

Think About It

1. How can you tell if an animal is an insect?
2. What else do you know about insects?

How Do Animals Grow?

Animals and Their Young

You will need

animal picture cards

paper and pencil

Animals and Their Young		
Animal	Same	Different
cats	Both have ears. Both are orange.	One is big. One is small.

1 Match the picture cards. Put each young animal with the adult.

2 Make a chart. Compare the young animal and the adult.

3 Tell how each young animal is like the adult. Tell how it is different.

Science Skill

When you compare the pictures, you tell how they are the same and different.

How Different Kinds of Animals Grow

These young animals will change as they get older. They will grow to look like their parents.

bunny

chick

Ways Animals Begin Life

Rabbits are small when they are born. Their eyes are closed. They can not walk or hop until they are older.

just born

8 days old

■ **How do the chick and the rabbit change in different ways?**

Chicks **hatch**, or break out of eggs. Their eyes are open. Soon they can walk and peck for food.

just hatched

8 days old

8 weeks old

adult

8 weeks old

adult

Animals Care for Their Young

Some animals feed their young. Later they teach them how to find food.

robins

brown bears

■ How do these animals make sure their young have food?

Some animals lick their young to clean them. Later they show them how to clean themselves.

chimpanzees

Some animals stay close to their young to keep them warm. Others keep their young warm in pouches.

■ **How do these penguins keep their baby warm?**

emperor penguins

Think About It

1. What are two ways that animals begin life?
2. How do all young animals change as they grow?

How Does a Butterfly Grow?

A Butterfly's Life

You will need

box

caterpillar

paper and pencil

1 Keep your caterpillar in a warm place.

2 Observe your caterpillar every day for three weeks. Draw it each time.

3 How did your caterpillar change? Share what happened.

Science Skill

When you use your senses to observe, you find out how the caterpillar changes.

How a Butterfly Grows

A butterfly is an insect. It hatches from an egg. It changes many times before it grows colorful wings. What do all insects have?

monarch butterfly

From Caterpillar to Butterfly

A butterfly begins life as an egg. A tiny caterpillar, or **larva**, hatches from the egg. The caterpillar eats and grows.

1 egg

2 caterpillar, or larva

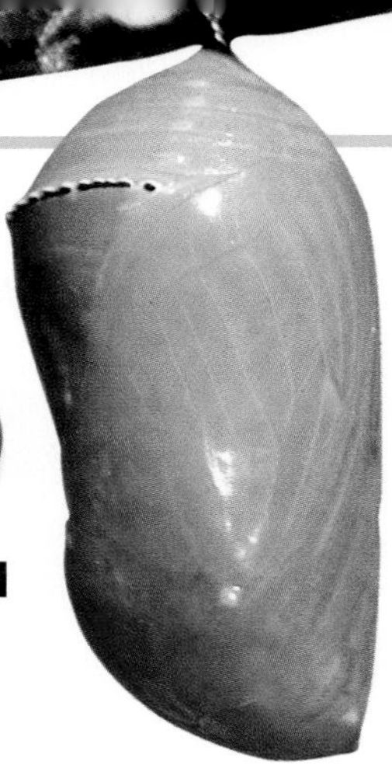

3 pupa

4 butterfly comes out

Then it stops eating. The caterpillar becomes a **pupa** and makes a hard covering.

Inside the covering, the pupa slowly changes. Finally a butterfly comes out and flies away.

5 adult butterfly

Wings Help Butterflies Keep Safe

Butterfly wings have different shapes and colors. Some wings look like leaves or flowers. These wings help butterflies hide.

Buckeye

Spring Azure

Tiger Swallowtail

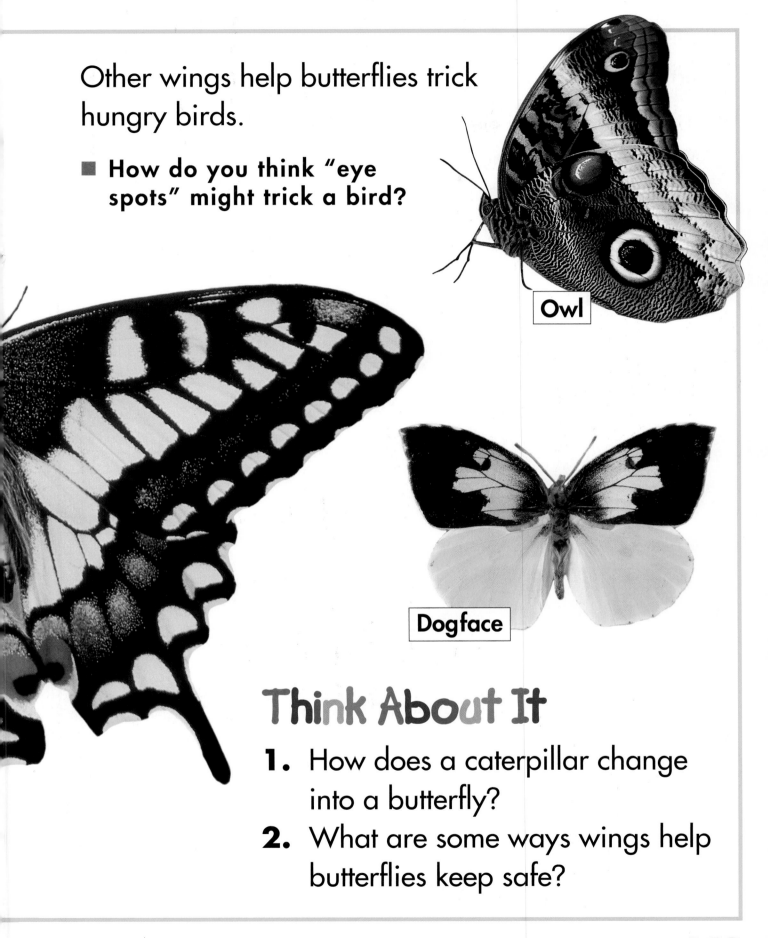

Other wings help butterflies trick hungry birds.

■ **How do you think "eye spots" might trick a bird?**

Owl

Dogface

Think About It

1. How does a caterpillar change into a butterfly?
2. What are some ways wings help butterflies keep safe?

How Does a Frog Grow?

A Frog's Life

You will need

picture cards

1 Put the picture cards in sequence. Show how you think a frog changes as it grows.

2 Tell why you put your cards in the order you did.

Science Skill

When you sequence the cards, you show what happens first, next, and last.

How a Frog Grows

A frog is an amphibian. It hatches from an egg. As it grows, it changes many times. When it is an adult, it has long back legs.

leopard frog

From Tadpole to Frog

Frogs lay their eggs in water. Young frogs, or **tadpoles**, hatch from the eggs. They have tails to move and gills to breathe in water. They grow.

■ How has this tadpole changed?

3
tadpole with back legs

2
tadpole

1
frog eggs

The tadpoles keep changing. They grow front legs. They get lungs to breathe air. Their tails get smaller. Then they look like little frogs. They climb onto land and grow bigger.

4 tadpole grows front legs, tail gets smaller

5 adult frog

Think About It

1. How does a tadpole change into a frog?
2. What body parts does a tadpole have that a frog does not have?

 Movement/Drama Link

Move Like a Frog

These children think about a time in a frog's life. Then they move to show what that time is like.

Write

Find an open space on the floor. Show what a frog does as an egg, a tadpole, or an adult frog. Then write about how frogs change.

Math Link

Find Symmetry

Look at this butterfly's wings. Find the two parts that match. Use your finger to trace a line between the matching parts.

Think and Do

Make a butterfly with wings that match.

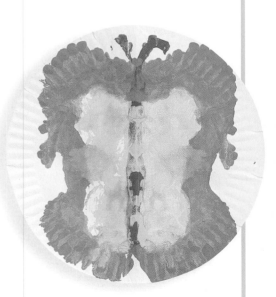

Fold a paper plate in half. Open the plate, and paint patterns on one half. While the paint is wet, press the two halves together. Then open the plate.

How are the two parts the same?

Tell What You Know

1. Tell how these animals are the same.
Then tell how they are different.

Vocabulary

Tell which picture goes best with each word.

2. mammal

3. reptile

4. amphibian

5. insect

6. gills

7. pupa

8. tadpole

9. hatch

10. larva

a.

b.

c.

d.

e.

f.

g.

h.

i.

Using Science Skills

11. Classify Make a graph to show groups of animals. Find pictures of animals. Classify your pictures to make a graph like this one.

Animal Groups

Number

Insects | Amphibians | Mammals | Fish | Reptiles | Birds

Kinds of Animals

12. Sequence A butterfly changes as it grows. Write the words in sequence to show how this insect changes.

adult butterfly

larva

egg

pupa

Activities
for Home or School

Senses Game

Get a box and put in different things. Ask your family or classmates to close their eyes. Have them use touch and hearing to guess each thing.

Nature Walk

Take a nature walk with your class or with family members. Draw or write about what you observe.

Growing and Changing

Look at photos of yourself with a family member. Talk about how you have changed.

Observe a Pet

With an adult, find a pet to observe. Draw or write about the animal.

What does the pet look like?

What does it eat and drink?

PLACES TO VISIT

The National Zoo, Washington, D.C.

At the National Zoo you can learn about animals and plants from around the world. You can see how animals and plants help each other. You can also see how the zoo helps endangered animals.

Plan Your Own Expedition

Visit a zoo or park near you. Or log on to The Learning Site.

 GO ONLINE www.harcourtschool.com

Living Together

UNIT B LIFE SCIENCE

Living Together

UNIT EXPERIMENT

Animal Coverings

How do body coverings help animals?
Plan and do a test to find out.

CHAPTER 1

Plants and Animals Need One Another

Vocabulary

shelter

enrich

pollen

product

Did You Know?
Some animals such as the clownfish use other animals for shelter.

Did You Know?
Ragweed **pollen** has sharp points that make people sneeze.

How Do Animals Need Plants?

Investigate

How Small Animals Use Plants

You will need

timer or watch   string loop   paper and pencil

1 Go outside with your class. Observe animals and plants inside your string loop.

2 Observe and record for five minutes. How are animals using plants?

3 Share what you observed.

Science Skill

As you observe, use your senses of sight, hearing, and smell to help you.

How Animals Need Plants

Many animals need plants for food. Some animals use plants to hide in or to make nests for their young.

plant

rabbit

Animals Need Plants for Food

Some animals eat only plants. Rabbits eat the tops and the roots of carrot plants. Caterpillars eat leaves.

■ **What does this cow eat?**

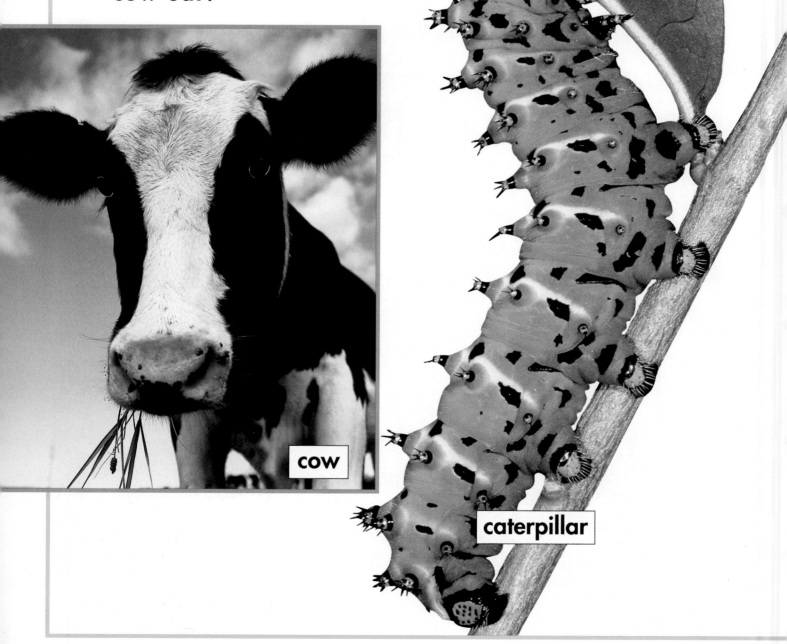

cow

caterpillar

Some animals eat other animals as well as plants. A toucan eats insects as well as fruit. A raccoon eats both fish and berries.

■ **What is this raccoon eating?**

raccoon

toucan

Other Ways Animals Need Plants

Some animals need plants for shelter. A **shelter** is a place where an animal can be safe.

African leopard

■ How does the tree help this leopard keep safe?

Many animals that live in the soil need plants for shelter. They may live inside rotting logs. They eat bits of dead plants.

termites

Some animals make nests with parts of plants. A bird may use grass. An alligator uses leaves and strong reeds.

oriole

alligator

deer mice

■ **What do mice use to make a nest?**

Think About It

1. What are some ways animals need plants?

2. What animals eat only plants? What animals eat other animals as well as plants?

How Do Animals Help Plants?

Investigate

How Seeds Stick to Animals

You will need

Styrofoam ball

glue

Velcro, cotton, and sandpaper

1 Look at this picture. How might these seeds stick to animals?

2 Plan a model of a seed that sticks. Choose materials to glue to the ball.

3 Investigate your materials. Which ones stick to the cotton? The cotton is like animal fur.

Science Skill

To investigate how seeds stick to animals, make a plan to try out different ideas. Follow your plan.

How Animals Help Plants

Some animals carry seeds to new places. Some help make the soil better for plants. Others help flowers make seeds.

Animals Carry Seeds

A seed may stick to a cat's fur. The seed may be carried far from the plant. When the seed falls off, it may grow into a new plant.

seed bur

Animals Help Make Soil Better

earthworm

A worm eats dead plants. Its waste helps **enrich** the soil, or make the soil better for plants.

■ **What things are these animals doing that help plants?**

Animals Help Plants Make Seeds

Flowers have a powder called **pollen** that helps them make seeds. A butterfly carries pollen from flower to flower. The pollen falls off. Those flowers use the pollen to make seeds.

butterfly

Think About It

1. How do small animals make the soil better for plants?

2. How do animals help plants grow new plants?

How Do We Need Plants and Animals?

Things People Use

You will need

picture cards

1 Which pictures show things made from plants? Which are from animals?

2 Classify the cards. Sort them into groups.

3 Share your groups. Tell why each thing belongs.

Science Skill
When you classify the things on the cards, you group them to show ways they are the same.

How People Need Plants and Animals

People need plants and animals for food, clothing, and shelter. Plants and animals also add beauty to people's lives.

What People Need Plants For

People need shelter and clothing. They use plants to make many products. A **product** is something that people make from other things.

cotton shirt

cotton bolls

■ **Where did the lumber come from to make this house?**

People eat parts of plants. Celery is the stem of a plant. Peanut butter is made from peanuts, the seeds of a plant.

■ **What plant do you like to eat?**

People also use plants to make products they need in their homes.

What People Need Animals For

People use animals for food. Many people eat beef, pork, chicken, and fish. Eggs and milk are also foods from animals.

■ **What parts of this breakfast come from animals? What parts come from plants?**

People use wool from sheep to make clothing. Coats and sweaters may be made with wool.

Guide Dog Trainer

Some people keep animals as pets. Others need animals as helpers. Guide dog trainers work with some dogs. They teach them to help blind people.

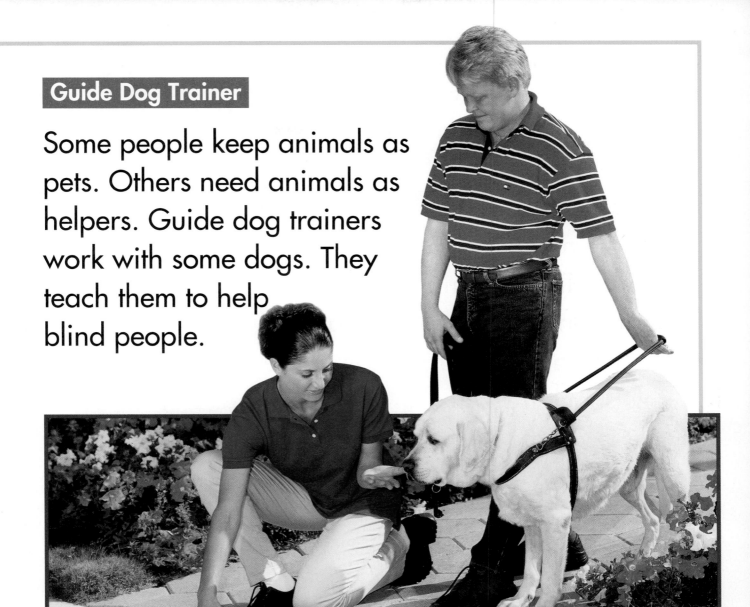

Think About It

1. What are some ways people need plants?

2. What are some ways people need animals?

Math Link

Measure Snacks Made from Plants

People make snacks from plants. They mix nuts, dried fruits, and cereal to make a tasty treat. Stores may call this snack *trail mix.*

Write

Make a snack from plants. Measure one cup each of granola, raisins, and nuts into a bowl. Mix them. Eat your trail mix snack. Then write about a different snack you can make using plants.

Social Studies Link

Keeping a Custom

Long ago, some African Americans in South Carolina made baskets like this one. They wove them from plants. This woman keeps the custom. She weaves a basket as people did long ago.

Think and Do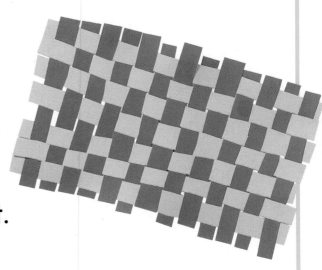

Paper comes from plants. It is made from the wood of trees. Use strips of colored paper to weave a place mat.

Tell What You Know

1. Tell how animals and people can use these plants to meet their needs.

Vocabulary

Tell which picture goes with each word. Then use the word to tell about the picture.

a.   **b.**

2. enrich

3. shelter

4. pollen

5. product

c.   **d.**

Using Science Skills

6. **Classify** Collect pictures of different kinds of foods. Put the foods that come from plants in one group. Put the foods that come from animals in another group.

   What foods can you find that come from both plants and animals?

7. **Observe** Make a chart about the ways you use plants and animals. Observe ways you use them at school. Draw pictures in your chart.

Ways I Use Plants and Animals			
	Food	Clothing	Beauty
Plants			
Animals			

A Place to Live

Vocabulary

forest
desert
rain forest
ocean
algae

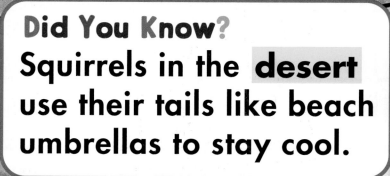

Did You Know?
Squirrels in the **desert** use their tails like beach umbrellas to stay cool.

Did You Know?
A plant called **algae** is used to make ice cream.

What Lives in a Forest?

Forest Trees

You will need

dark crayon

pencil and paper

1 Go outside. Find a tree. Draw one of its leaves.

2 Make a rubbing of the tree's bark.

3 Compare your drawing and rubbing with a classmate's.

Science Skill
When you compare drawings and rubbings, look for ways the trees are the same and different.

Forests

A **forest** is a place where many trees grow. A forest floor is shady. The soil stays moist.

forest

Forest Plants and Animals

Some trees grow tall in a forest. Their high leaves catch the sunlight they need to make food.

Berry bushes and mountain laurels need less sunlight than trees. They can grow below the trees.

berry bushes

mountain laurel

Many animals find food and shelter in a forest. Wood thrushes find safe places to build their nests. Box turtles eat worms for food.

wood thrushes

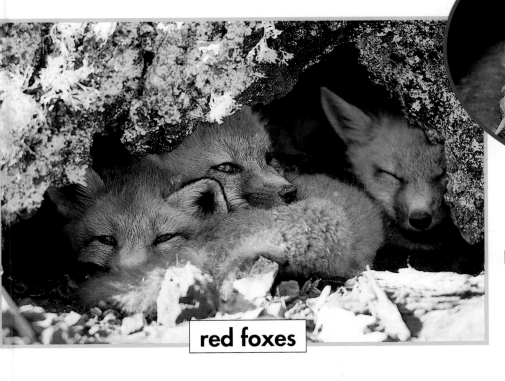
red foxes

■ **How are the foxes meeting their needs?**

Think About It

1. What is a forest?
2. How do plants and animals in a forest meet their needs?

box turtle

What Lives in the Desert?

Desert Leaves

You will need

2 paper clips

water

wax paper

2 paper-towel leaf shapes

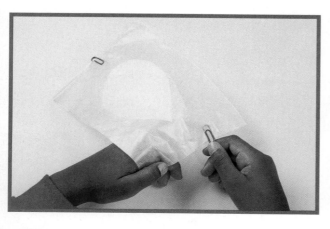

1 Make both leaf shapes damp. Put one shape on wax paper. Fold the paper over. Clip it.

2 Put both leaves in the sunlight. Check them after an hour.

3 Which leaf holds water longer? Draw a conclusion.

Science Skill
To draw a conclusion about desert leaves, think about your leaf with the waxy coat and the other leaf.

Deserts

A **desert** is a dry place. It gets lots of sunlight and little rain. Only a few kinds of plants and animals can live there.

desert

Desert Plants and Animals

Desert plants can hold water to use when they need it. Some, like the yucca, have thick leaves with a waxy coat. Others hold water in their thick stems.

cactus wren

yucca

beavertail cactus

Most deserts are hot. Desert animals have ways to stay cool and get water. Some, like the armadillo, stay in the shade. They look for food at night when it is cooler. Others, like the kangaroo rat, get water from their food.

■ **How do many of these animals stay cool?**

armadillo

rattlesnake

kangaroo rat

Think About It

1. What is a desert?
2. How do plants and animals live in a desert?

What Lives in a Rain Forest?

Investigate

Rain Forest Plants

You will need

seeds

2 wet cotton balls

film cans and lid with hole

plastic and rubber band

wet cotton ball

seeds

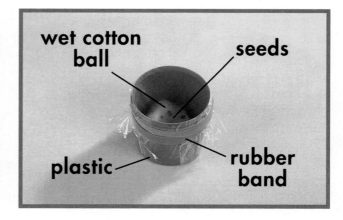

wet cotton ball

seeds

plastic

rubber band

1 Some rain forest plants get little light. Make a model of a rain forest like this one. Close lid.

2 Plants in open areas get more light. Make a model of an open area.

3 Set both models in the sun for 5 days. Tell how the cotton changes.

Science Skill
To communicate how the forests grew, draw and share pictures of what you observed.

Rain Forests

A **rain forest** is wet all year. Most rain forests are warm, too. Rain and warm weather help trees and other plants grow. Animals use the plants to meet their needs.

rain forest

Rain Forest Animals and Plants

Animals live at different levels of the rain forest. Macaws live near the treetops. They find fruit to eat. Sloths hang from the middle of trees. They find shelter there and plants to eat.

macaw

three-toed sloths

orchid

Rain forest plants also live at different levels. Most grow from roots in the soil. Some, like the orchid, grow from roots halfway up trees. They get the light they need there.

bromeliad

Think About It

1. What is a rain forest?
2. Why are plants found at different levels in the rain forest?

■ Where does the rain forest plant called a bromeliad live?

What Lives in the Ocean?

Ocean Animals

You will need

ocean picture cards

1 Which ocean pictures show fish? Which show other animals?

2 Classify the animals. Put them in groups.

3 Share your groups. Talk about other ways to classify the animals.

Science Skill

When you classify the animals, you group them to show ways they are the same.

B38

Oceans

An **ocean** is a large, deep body of salt water. Oceans cover three fourths of the Earth.

ocean

Ocean Animals and Plants

Many kinds of animals live in the ocean. Some fish eat **algae**, which are like plants. Some algae are called seaweed.

seaweed

■ **What is the fish using the algae for?**

bottle-nosed dolphin

green sea turtle

starfish

Ocean animals can find what they need in ocean waters. Dolphins' strong tails help them swim fast to catch fish.

Sea turtles use their flippers to swim and catch food.

■ **How do you think a starfish's shape helps it get food?**

Think About It

1. What is an ocean?
2. How do ocean animals get what they need to live?

Math Link

Observe Leaf Patterns

You can find leaf patterns on a tree twig. A tree grows leaves the same way again and again. The leaves make a pattern.

Think and Do

Look at a tree twig with leaves. Observe how the leaves grow in a pattern. Draw a picture that shows the pattern.

A Scientist Investigates the Ocean

Sylvia Earle is a marine biologist, a scientist who studies life in the ocean. She dives deep to find out about ocean plants and animals. She also helps people learn about the ocean.

Write

Choose a plant or an animal that lives in the ocean. Read books to learn more about it. Write about the plant or animal.

Great Blue Whale

Krill

The great blue whale is the largest animal.

Tell What You Know

1. Tell about where each animal lives.

Vocabulary

Tell which picture goes with the word or words.

2. algae

3. rain forest

4. ocean

5. desert

6. forest

a.   **b.**   **c.**

d.   **e.**

Using Science Skills

7. Classify Read the clues. Name each plant or animal. Tell where it lives.

   a. This plant has thorns that keep animals from eating it. It has a waxy coat to keep water in.

   b. This animal has fins for swimming. It uses algae for food and shelter.

   c. This plant lives halfway up on trees. It needs a warm, wet place.

8. Compare Look at the graph. Tell which place gets the most rain in a month.

How Much Rain Falls in a Month?	
Temperate Forest	⬭ ⬭ ⬭ ⬭ ⬭
Rain Forest	⬭ ⬭ ⬭ ⬭ ⬭ ⬭ ⬭ ⬭ ⬭ ⬭ ⬭ ⬭ ⬭ ⬭
Desert	⬭

Each ⬭ equals 2 centimeters.

Activities
for Home or School

What Do Worms Need?

1. Put two kinds of soil and two worms in a covered box.

2. In two hours, check where the worms are.

3. What do the worms need? Talk about what you observe.

Make a Bird Feeder

1. Cut the top off of a plastic jug. Punch holes on both sides.

2. Tie string through the holes.

3. Pour some birdseed inside. Hang outdoors.

4. Observe birds that eat the seeds.

Rain Forest in a Jar

1. Put pebbles, soil, and plants in a jar.

2. Water the plants. Put the lid on the jar.

3. Put the jar where it gets light but not strong sun.

4. Wait one day. Observe. How is this like a rain forest?

Stems That Store Water

1. Observe the stem tubes, or small dots, on a cut celery stalk.

2. Set the stalk in an empty cup. Put it in the sun until it droops.

3. Add water to the cup. Put it in the refrigerator. The next day, tell what happened and why.

stem tubes

PLACES TO VISIT

Sea Lion Caves, Florence, Oregon

At Sea Lion Caves you can view where sea lions live. You can see how these caves and the ocean provide these animals with a place to live.

Plan Your Own Expedition

Visit a zoo or park near you. Or log on to The Learning Site.

 www.harcourtschool.com

About Our Earth

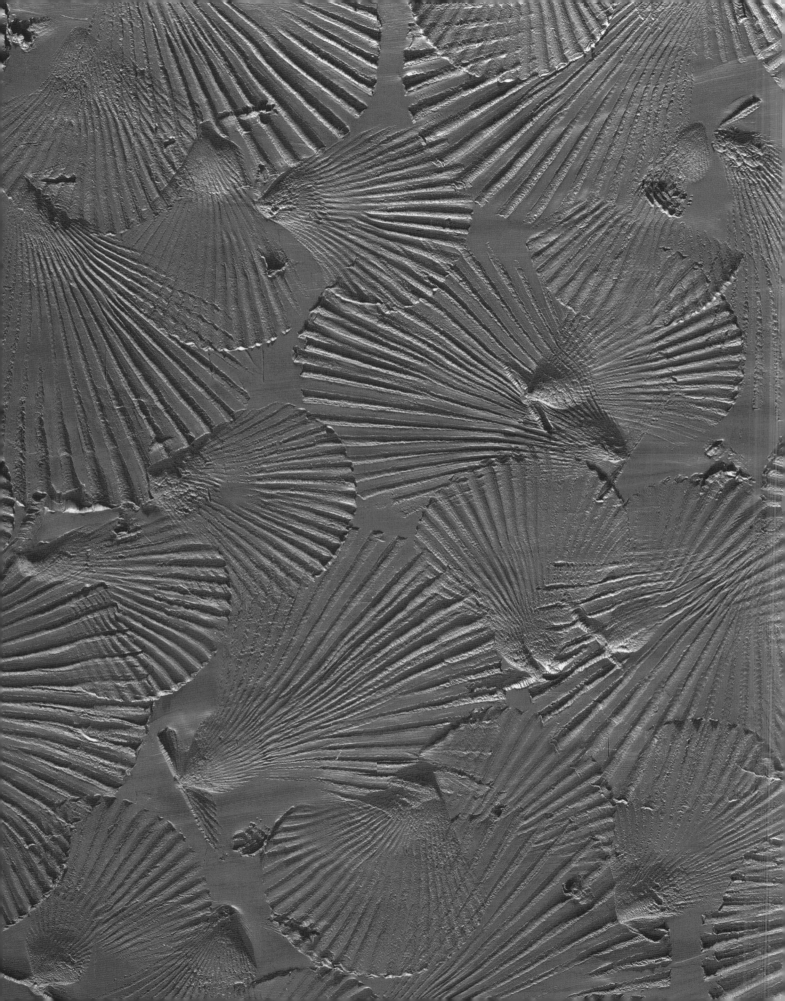

About Our Earth

UNIT EXPERIMENT

Clean Air

Where is air the cleanest?
Plan and do a test to find out.

Earth's Land

Vocabulary

rock

sand

fossil

extinct

Did You Know?
Sometimes a whole forest
can become a **fossil**.

Did You Know?
Chalk is **rock** made from the shells of tiny sea animals.

What Can We Observe About Rocks?

Investigate

Ways to Classify Rocks

You will need

hand lens

different rocks

paper and pencil

Rocks			
Red			

1 Observe each rock with the hand lens. Feel each rock. Write how the rocks look and feel.

2 Make a chart. Classify your rocks on the chart.

Science Skill

When you classify your rocks, you group them by ways they are the same.

Rocks

A **rock** is a hard, nonliving thing that comes from the Earth. There are many kinds of rocks. People use rocks in different ways.

Different Kinds of Rocks

Some rocks are big, and some are small. Tiny broken pieces of rock are called **sand**. Rocks may be different colors. Some rocks are smooth. Others are rough.

sand

rose quartzite

lava

marble

obsidian

■ How are these rocks the same? How are they different?

limestone

People use rocks to build homes and walls. They melt sand to make glass.

■ **How have these people used rocks?**

Think About It

1. What are rocks?

2. What ways do people use rocks?

What Are Fossils?

Investigate

A Shell Fossil

You will need

       craft stick

a shell   petroleum jelly   sand in a pan   glue   measuring cup   craft stick

1 You can make a model of a fossil. Mix an equal amount of sand and glue in a pan.

2 Rub the shell with petroleum jelly. Press it firmly into the mix.

3 Let the glue dry. Pull the shell out of the sand. What do you see?

Science Skill

You can make a model to help you understand how fossils form.

C8

Fossils

Plants and animals lived on Earth long ago, just as they do today. Scientists have found parts and imprints of these plants and animals. The parts and imprints of a plant or an animal that lived long ago are called **fossils**.

Animal Fossils

Fossils form where animals live. This starfish lived in the sea. After it died, mud covered it. Over millions of years, the mud turned to rock and the starfish became a fossil.

starfish fossil

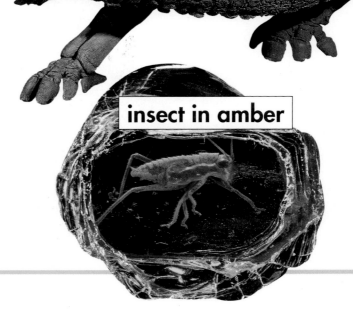

fossil

The insect lived on land. Sap from a tree covered the insect. The sap hardened, and the insect became a fossil.

insect in amber

Plant Fossils

Plants or plant parts can also become fossils. A leaf may become a fossil. A cone may become a fossil.

fossil

cone fossil

Think About It

1. What are fossils?
2. What living things can become fossils?

leaf fossil

What Have We Learned from Fossils?

Investigate

Animals Then and Now

You will need

picture cards

1 You can compare animal fossils with animals of today. You and a partner each take one of the sets of cards.

2 Your partner will put down a card that shows an animal fossil or an animal of today. Put down the matching card.

3 Take turns. Play until all the animal cards are matched.

Science Skill
When you compare animals of long ago and today, look for ways they are the same.

What We Can Find Out from Fossils

We can learn from fossils. We can tell how big an animal was. We can see how many legs it had.

ground sloth

Kinds of Fossils

There are fossils of large and small plants and animals. There are also fossils of land and sea plants and animals.

Kinds of plants or animals that are no longer living are **extinct**.

extinct sea animal

extinct scallop

living scallop

extinct fern

living fern

People can learn how plants and animals have changed by comparing them with fossils. We can use artists' drawings to compare extinct elephants to living elephants.

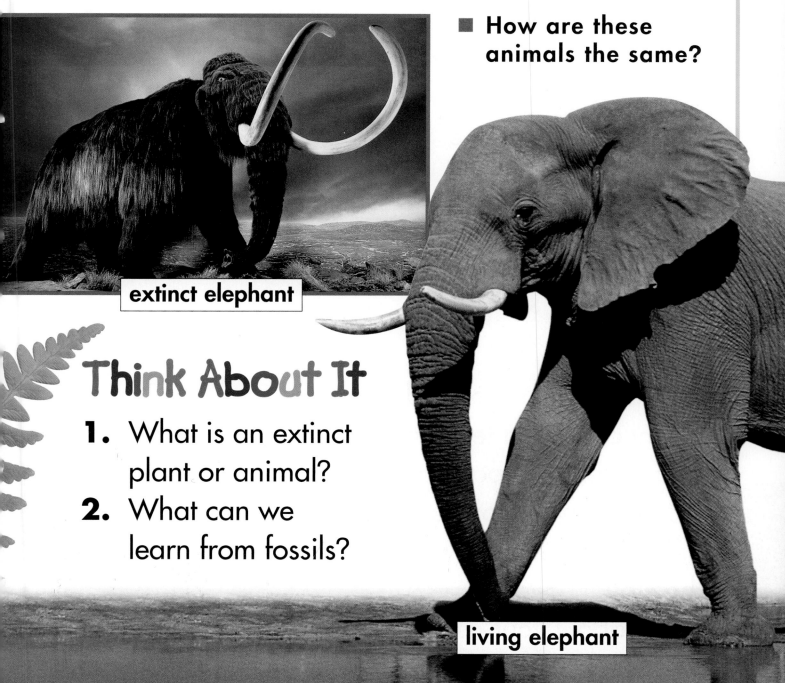

extinct elephant

■ **How are these animals the same?**

Think About It

1. What is an extinct plant or animal?
2. What can we learn from fossils?

living elephant

 Art/Career Link

Scientists Work to Save Ancient Art

Cave paintings were made thousands of years ago. They show animals that were alive then. After scientists discovered the paintings, people came to see them. Because some people harmed the paintings, now only scientists can study them.

Write

People of long ago used bright colors made from rocks and minerals to paint animals that lived then. You can paint animals that live now. Show them on the wall of a cave. Write about your cave.

Measure Mass

Long ago, people used rocks or stones to measure mass. They put an object on one side of a balance. They added rocks to the other side until the two sides balanced. The number of rocks told the mass of the object.

Think and Do

Collect some rocks that are about the same size. Use a balance to measure the mass of some objects.

Tell What You Know

1. Tell what you know about each picture.

Vocabulary

Tell which picture goes with each word.

2. sand

3. rock

4. fossil

5. extinct

a.   **b.**

c.   **d.**

Using Science Skills

6. Make a Model Make a model of a fossil. Mix glue and food coloring. Use a toothpick to put a "fossil" into the glue. Let the glue dry.

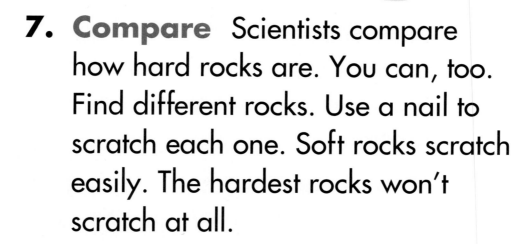

7. Compare Scientists compare how hard rocks are. You can, too. Find different rocks. Use a nail to scratch each one. Soft rocks scratch easily. The hardest rocks won't scratch at all.

Which rock is the hardest? Which is the softest? Tell how you know.

What Are Natural Resources?

The World Around You

You will need

paper and pencil

Things I Saw Outdoors	
animals	
plants	
water	
land	
soil	

1 Make a chart like this one. Then go outdoors. Gather data about what you observe.

2 Look for the things on your chart. Make a tally mark to record what you see.

3 Compare with a classmate. Did you see the same things or different things?

Science Skill
To gather data, observe and record what you see.

Natural Resources

A **natural resource** is something found in nature that people can use. Plants and animals are natural resources. Land, water, and air are also natural resources.

Forests

Forests are a natural resource. People use the trees in forests for many things. Some trees grow nuts that are good to eat. The wood from many trees is used to make furniture. What other kinds of things are made from wood?

hickory nuts

hickory tree

hickory chair

Soil

Soil is a natural resource. People use soil to grow crops for food. Lettuce, carrots, and corn are some of the crops people grow in soil.

lettuce

Minerals

Some cooking pots are made from copper. Copper is a natural resource. Aluminum is another natural resource. It is used to make cans. Garnets are a natural resource used to make jewelry.

garnet

copper

aluminum mineral

Aluminum cans, copper pots, and garnet jewelry are made from **minerals**. A mineral is one kind of nonliving thing that is found in nature. Minerals are a natural resource.

Think About It

1. What are some natural resources?
2. What is a mineral?

Where Is Air on Earth?

Air in a Bag

You will need

plastic bag

1 Pull an open bag toward you. Then hold the top of the bag closed.

2 Squeeze the bag. What do you observe? Poke a hole in the bag.

3 What was in the bag? How did you infer that?

Science Skill

When you infer, you use what you observe and know to make a good guess.

 **Learn About**

Where Air Is

Air is a natural resource. We can not see, taste, or smell it. Yet air is all around.

■ **What is lifting up the kite in this picture?**

Where Is Fresh Water Found?

Investigate

Making Salt Water Fresh

You will need

rubber band

salt, bucket, and sand

marbles and plastic wrap

2 cups and water

1 Mix some salt in water. Taste the water. Pour the water into the bucket. Throw away used cups.

2 Put another cup in the bottom of the bucket. Cover. Put marbles on top.

3 Place the bucket in the sun. Wait two hours. Take the cup out. Taste the water. Draw a conclusion.

Science Skill

To draw a conclusion, think about what you observed and what you know about water.

Fresh Water

Water is another natural resource. Water that is not salty is called **fresh water**. Rain is fresh water. Rain makes puddles or sinks into the ground.

stream

Where Fresh Water Comes From

Rain and melted snow run down mountains. They may form a **stream**, a small body of moving water.

The stream may flow into a **river**, a larger body of moving water. The river flows into a lake. A **lake** is a body of water with land all around it.

river

mountains

lake

People need clean fresh water for drinking, cooking, and washing.

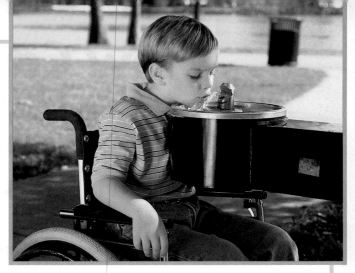

Water Testers

Water from lakes and rivers is cleaned. Then people can drink it. A water tester checks water. The clean water flows through pipes to people's homes.

Think About It

1. What is fresh water?
2. Where do we find fresh water?

Activities
for Home or School

Measure and Group Rocks

1. Make a balance like this one.

2. Put 10 pennies in one cup.

3. Put a rock in the other cup.

4. Which rocks have more mass than the pennies? Group them.

Make Rock Art

1. You can make rock art as people did long ago. Find a rock with a flat part.

2. Use a toothpick to paint a picture on the flat part. Draw something that lives today as people did long ago.

3. Tell about your rock art.

How Much Air Is in a Breath?

1. Take a big breath.
2. Let it out by blowing into a balloon.
3. With your fingers, hold the end of the balloon closed. Observe how much air you breathed out.
4. Compare balloon breaths to a classmate's or family member's.

Visit a Park

1. With your class or family members, visit a park.
2. Observe how land is being used.
3. Draw a picture that shows what you observed.
4. Share your drawing.

Falls of the Ohio State Park, Clarksville, Indiana

At this park by the Ohio River, you can see the fossils of animals and plants that lived long ago. You can learn more about these animals and plants.

Plan Your Own Expedition

Visit a museum or a place near you that has fossils. Or log on to The Learning Site.

 www.harcourtschool.com

Weather, the Sky, and Seasons

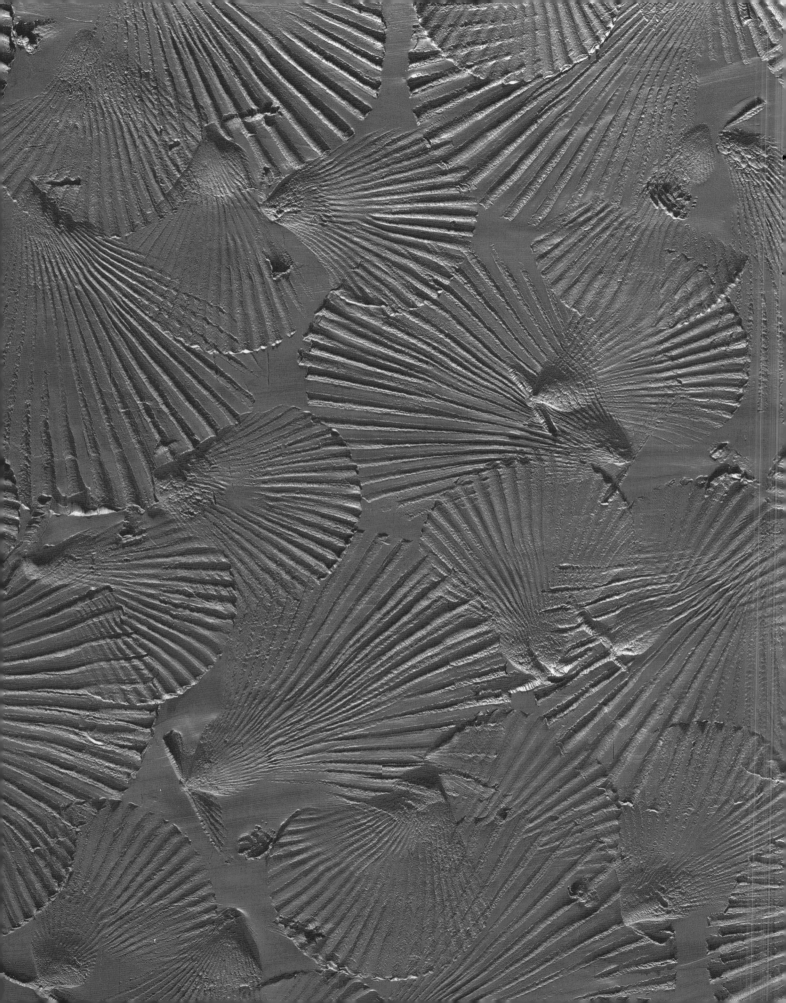

Weather, the Sky, and Seasons

UNIT EXPERIMENT

Heat and Water

What does sunlight do to water?
Plan and do a test to find out.

Measuring Weather

Vocabulary

weather
temperature
thermometer
wind
water cycle
evaporate
water vapor
condense

Did You Know?
You don't have to have rainy **weather** to get lightning.

Did You Know?
A landsailer can go more than 100 miles an hour in the **wind**.

What Is Weather?

Weather Conditions

You will need

paper

markers

Daily Weather				
Monday	Tuesday	Wednesday	Thursday	Friday

1 Observe the changes in weather for two weeks.

2 Make a chart. Draw or write what you observe on your chart.

3 Compare the daily weather changes you observed.

Science Skill

When you compare the things you observed, tell how they are the same and different.

Weather

It may be hot or cold outside. It may be sunny, cloudy, or rainy. All these words tell about weather. The **weather** is what the air outside is like.

rain gauge

Different Kinds of Weather

When the air outside changes, the weather changes. The weather may be hot one day and cool the next.

One day may be cloudy and rainy. The next day may be clear and sunny. One day may be very windy. Another day may be calm.

■ **How are these kinds of weather different?**

Meteorologist

Current Weather

Gulf of Mexico

People like to know what the weather will be. They check weather reports made by a meteorologist. A meteorologist is a scientist who studies weather.

Think About It

1. What is weather?

2. How can weather change from day to day?

What Is Temperature?

Investigate

Measuring Air Temperature

You will need

thermometer

paper and pencil

red crayon

1 Draw and label two thermometers.

2 Measure and record the air temperature in the classroom.

3 Put the thermometer outside for 5 minutes. Measure and record the air temperature.

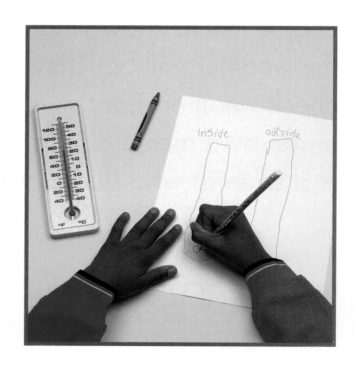

4 Compare the temperatures.

Science Skill
To measure temperature with a thermometer, read the number next to the top of the red line.

Temperature

The **temperature** is the measure of how hot or cold something is. Temperature is measured with a tool called a **thermometer**.

thermometer

■ **What is the temperature on the thermometer?**

Different Temperatures

The temperature of the air changes from day to day. It also changes as the seasons change. Sometimes it is so low that water freezes. Sometimes it is so high that an ice pop melts quickly.

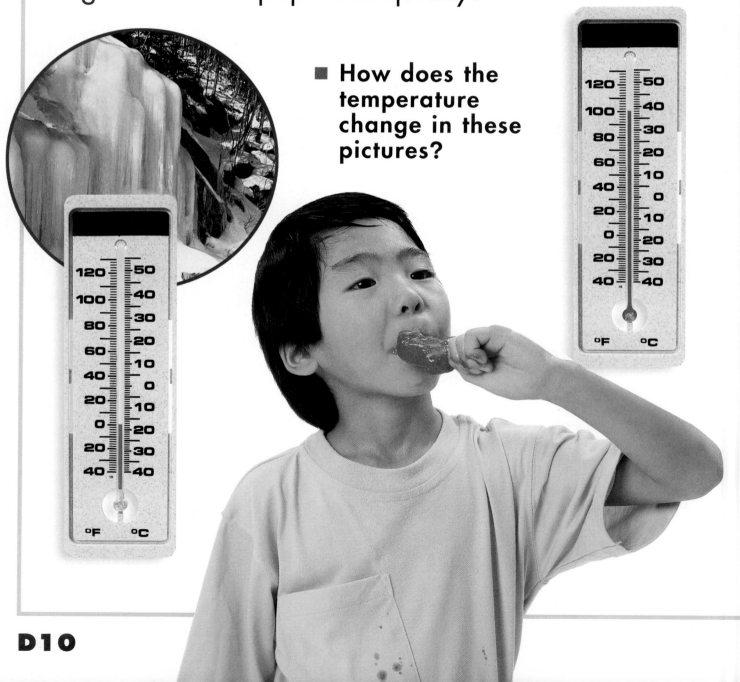

■ **How does the temperature change in these pictures?**

Air temperature may also change during the day. In the daytime the sun warms the air. The temperature goes up.

At night the sun does not warm the air. The temperature goes down, and the air feels cooler.

daytime

early evening

■ How are the temperatures different here? Why?

Think About It

1. What is a thermometer? How do you use it?
2. What is temperature? How does it change?

What Is Wind?

Investigate

Wind Direction

You will need

drinking straw

round toothpick

paper triangle

tape

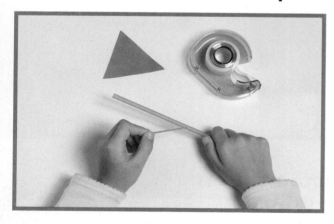

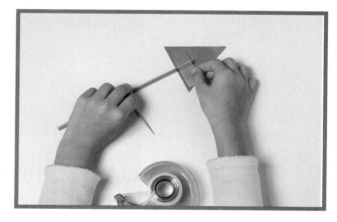

1 Make a wind vane. Poke the toothpick through the straw.

CAUTION Be careful. Toothpicks are sharp.

2 Tape the triangle to the straw. Go outdoors. Hold up the toothpick.

3 Observe the wind's direction on two windy days.

Science Skill

To observe the wind's direction, check which way the triangle points.

Wind

Moving air is called **wind**. Wind can push things. It can push a sailboat across a lake or blow a wind vane.

wind vane

Different Kinds of Wind

Sometimes the wind blows gently. Sometimes it blows hard.

A flag can show how hard the wind is blowing. When the wind blows gently, a flag ripples. When it blows hard, a flag flies straight out.

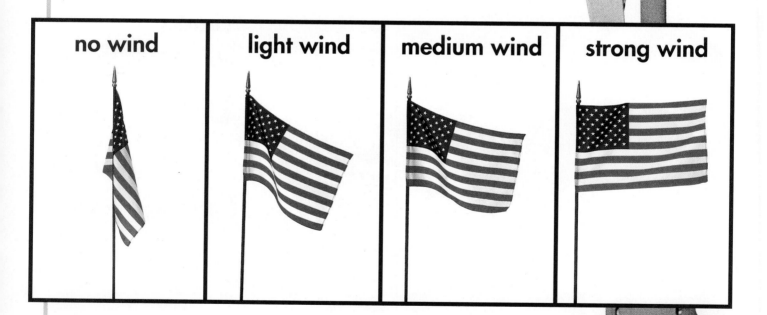

| no wind | light wind | medium wind | strong wind |

■ How does a flag show how hard the wind is blowing?

Strong wind turns windmills to make electricity. Sometimes wind can be too strong. The strong winds of a tornado can break up buildings.

Think About It

1. What is wind?
2. What are some different kinds of wind?

What Makes Clouds and Rain?

How Clouds Form

You will need

jar with lid

very warm water

ice cubes

1 Pour warm water into the jar. Wait. Pour out most of the water.

CAUTION Be careful. Water is hot!

2 Set the lid upside down on the jar. Observe the jar.

3 Put ice on the lid. Observe. Infer how clouds form.

Science Skill
To infer, first observe. Then think about what happened and draw a conclusion.

Clouds and Rain

Clouds are made up of many tiny drops of water. The drops may join and get heavier. When the drops get too heavy, they fall as rain.

 **Math Link**

Measure Air Temperature

Monday

Tuesday

In some places the air temperature changes a lot from day to day. In other places it changes only a little.

Temperature Changes	
Day of Week	Degrees Fahrenheit
Monday	60
Tuesday	40
Wednesday	

Write

Use a thermometer. Measure and record the temperature each day. Write about the temperature changes. Tell how weather changes make the temperature go up and down.

Weather Sayings

Long ago, sailors looked for patterns to predict the weather. This is one of their sayings.

<u>Red sky</u> at night,
Sailors' delight.
<u>Red sky</u> at morning,
Sailors take warning.

Sailors observed that a red sunset often comes before a sunny day. A red sunrise often comes before a rainy day.

Think and Do

Observe the weather for a week. Look for patterns. Make up a weather saying about a pattern you observe.

Tell What You Know

1. Tell what you know about the diagram. Use the words *water cycle, water vapor, evaporate,* and *condense.*

Vocabulary

Use each word to tell about the picture.

2.
weather

3.
temperature

4.
thermometer

5.
wind

Using Science Skills

6. Compare Make a chart about the weather. Observe and compare the weather in the morning and in the afternoon. Tell about the changes.

Today's Weather		
	Morning	Afternoon
How It Looks		
How It Sounds		
How It Feels		
How It Smells		

7. Observe Collect or draw pictures of clouds. Write a label for each picture.

Write a sentence that tells what each cloud looks like. Tell what weather you might have with that cloud.

CHAPTER 2

The Sky and the Seasons

Vocabulary

stars

sun

moon

rotates

season

spring

summer

fall

winter

Did You Know?
Many parts of the world have four seasons, but the tropical rain forest has only one **season**.

Did You Know?
When it is **summer** in North America, it is **winter** in South America.

What Can We See in the Sky?

 Investigate

The Sky

You will need

paper and pencil

The Sky	
Date	What I Saw

1 You can communicate about what you see in the sky. Make a chart like this one.

2 Go outdoors with your teacher. Observe the sky.

3 Draw pictures and write words to communicate what you see.

Science Skill

When you communicate, you can use a chart to tell about what you observe.

What We See in the Sky

There are many things to see in the sky in the daytime. You can see birds and clouds. You can see airplanes and helicopters. You may even see a hot-air balloon. You see different things at night.

Why Do We Have Day and Night?

Day and Night

You will need

globe

flashlight

labels

tape

1 Make a model of the sun and Earth. The flashlight is the sun. The globe is Earth. Tape on the labels.

2 Ask a partner to hold Earth. Shine the flashlight on Earth. The side facing the sun is having day. The other side is having night.

3 Tell how the model helps you see why we have day and night.

Science Skill

When you make a model, you can use it to find out why something happens.

Day

The sun gives off heat and light. The sun's heat warms Earth's land, air, and water. The sun's light makes the sky bright in the daytime.

Day and Night on Earth

Earth is always moving. Our planet **rotates**. This means it spins like a top. It takes 24 hours for Earth to rotate one time.

United States

day

As Earth rotates, sometimes the side we live on faces the sun. The sky is bright. We have daytime. Sometimes our side of Earth faces away from the sun. The sky is dark. We have night.

United States

night

Think About It

1. Why do we have day and night?
2. How does Earth's spinning give us day and night?

What Is Spring?

What Helps Seeds Sprout

You will need

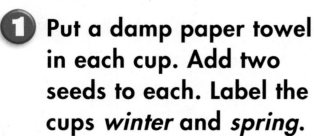

4 bean seeds

2 cups

mist bottle

paper towels

hand lens

1 Put a damp paper towel in each cup. Add two seeds to each. Label the cups *winter* and *spring*.

2 Put the *winter* cup in a cold, dark place. Put the *spring* cup in a warm, dark place.

3 Observe the seeds with the hand lens three days later. What can you infer?

Science Skill

To infer, first observe, and then think about what you see.

Spring

A **season** is a time of year. **Spring** is the season that follows winter. In spring, there are more hours of daylight. The air gets warmer. Spring rains fall.

spring summer fall winter

Plants and Animals in Spring

More daylight, warmer air, and spring rains help plants start growing. For farmers, spring is a good time to plant seeds.

■ How does spring help these plants start growing?

■ Which are the young animals?

Many animals give birth to their young in spring. Birds build nests and lay eggs. Lambs and other animals are born. The growing plants are food for many young animals.

Think About It

1. What is a season?
2. What is spring?

What Is Summer?

Colors That Can Keep You Cool

You will need

4 thermometers

4 colors of paper

stapler

clock

1 Fold and staple 4 color sheets of paper to make sleeves. Put a thermometer in each. Place in the sun.

2 Record the starting temperatures for each.

3 Wait 30 minutes. Record the temperatures again. Order from hottest to coolest.

Science Skill
To put the colors in order, start with the one with the hottest temperature. End with the coolest.

D38

Summer

Summer is the season that follows spring. Summer has the most hours of daylight of any season. In many places the air gets hot.

spring   summer   fall   winter

Plants and Animals in Summer

In summer, lots of sunlight helps plants grow leaves and flowers. Soon fruits begin to form and grow.

■ **What do these plants get in summer that helps them make fruit?**

In summer, young animals eat and grow. Young horses, called foals, become strong and fast.

Young birds lose their first feathers. They begin to look like adults.

Think About It

1. What is summer?
2. How is summer different from spring?

What Is Fall?

 Investigate

Storing Apples

You will need

apple rings

string

plastic bag

paper and pencil

1 Put some apple rings in the plastic bag. Store them on a shelf.

2 Hang the other apple rings on string. Don't let them touch.

3 Predict and record what will happen.

4 Wait one week. Record.

> **Science Skill**
>
> To predict which way to store apple rings is better, use what you know about food. Then decide.

Fall

The season that follows summer is **fall**.
In fall, there are fewer hours of daylight.
The air grows cool. In some places, leaves
change colors and drop to the ground.

spring summer fall winter

Plants and Animals in Fall

In fall, plants get less sunlight and stop growing bigger. They make seeds that will sprout next spring. Fruits and vegetables are ready to be picked.

■ **What made these plants stop growing bigger?**

When plants stop growing, animals have less food. Some animals move to places where there is more food. Others store food so they have something to eat in winter.

Think About It

1. What is fall?
2. How is fall different from summer?

What Is Winter?

Investigate

Keeping Warm in Cold Weather

You will need

plastic bag

container of ice water

things to keep your hand warm

1 Put your hand in the bag. Then put your hand in the ice water. Does the bag keep your hand warm?

2 What could you put in the bag to keep your hand warm? Choose some things to try.

3 Investigate your ideas by trying them. Which one works best?

Science Skill

To investigate how to keep your hand warm, try out each of your ideas.

Winter

Winter is the season that follows fall. There are fewer hours of daylight than in fall. In many places the air gets cold and snow falls.

spring   summer   fall   winter

Plants and Animals in Winter

In winter, days do not have many hours of sunlight. The branches of many trees and bushes are bare.

Some plants are resting. Some plants that made seeds are now dead.

Where winters are cold, animals can not find much food. Some eat food they stored in fall. Some sleep through the winter.

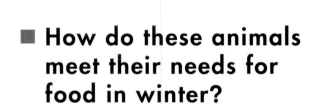 How do these animals meet their needs for food in winter?

Think About It

1. What is winter?
2. What are some ways animals live in winter?

Art Link

A Photographer Observes the Seasons

Ansel Adams was a photographer. Each season, he took pictures of his favorite places. His photographs help us see the beauty of the seasons.

Write

Draw pictures to show your favorite place in different seasons. Label each picture with the season it shows. Write about the season you like the most.

fall

winter

 **Math Link**

Read a Bar Graph

In a part of northern California, some seasons are wet and some are dry. This graph shows about how many inches or centimeters of rain fall in each season.

How Much Rain?												
Winter												
Spring												
Summer												
Fall												

inches   0   1   2   3   4   5   6   7   8   9   10   11

centimeters   5   10   15   20   25

Think and Do

Look at the bar graph. Which season is the wettest in northern California? Which is the driest?

Tell What You Know

1. Tell what you know about the pictures. Use the word *stars*, *sun*, *moon*, or *rotate* to tell about each one.

Vocabulary

Use each word to tell about the picture.

2.

season

3.

spring

4.

summer

5.

fall

6.

winter

Using Science Skills

7. **Order** Use four sheets of paper. On each, write the name of one of the seasons. Then draw the clothes you would wear. Put your sheets in order, beginning with summer.

8. **Predict and Investigate** Look at the colors of these shirts. Predict which color will stay the coolest in hot sun. Write your prediction. Use any color paper to investigate your idea.

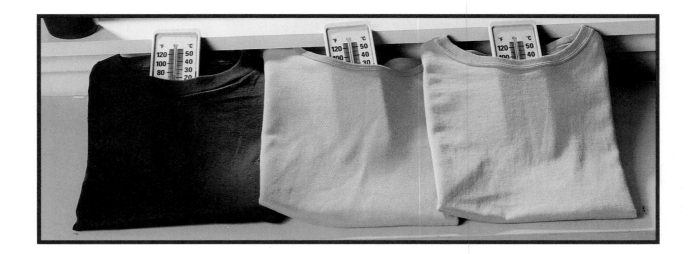

Activities
for Home or School

Make a Sail for a Car

Put a paper sail on a toy car. Blow on the sail to make the car move. What could you do to make a better sail? Try your ideas.

Investigate Water Vapor

1. With an adult present, blow into a small plastic bag.

2. Observe the water drops inside. They come from the water vapor in your breath.

3. Put the bag in a freezer for five minutes. Tell what happens.

4. Put the bag in the sun for five minutes. Tell what happens.

Make a Four Seasons Poster

Fold a big sheet of paper into four parts. Label each part for a different season. Add pictures of things you like to do in each season. Talk about how the weather changes.

Find Seasons in a Closet

What clothes do people wear at different times of the year where you live? Brainstorm ideas. Write a list that shows at least two things for each season.

PLACES TO VISIT

The Franklin Institute Science Museum, Philadelphia, Pennsylvania

You can learn more about Earth's weather at this science museum. You can see how weather is studied. You can also find out how to take your own weather measurements.

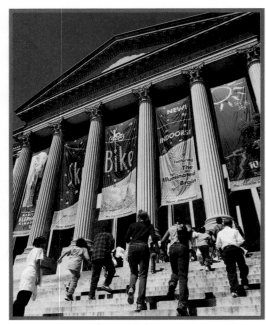

Plan Your Own Expedition

Visit a museum or weather station near you. Or log on to The Learning Site.

GO ONLINE www.harcourtschool.com

Matter and Energy

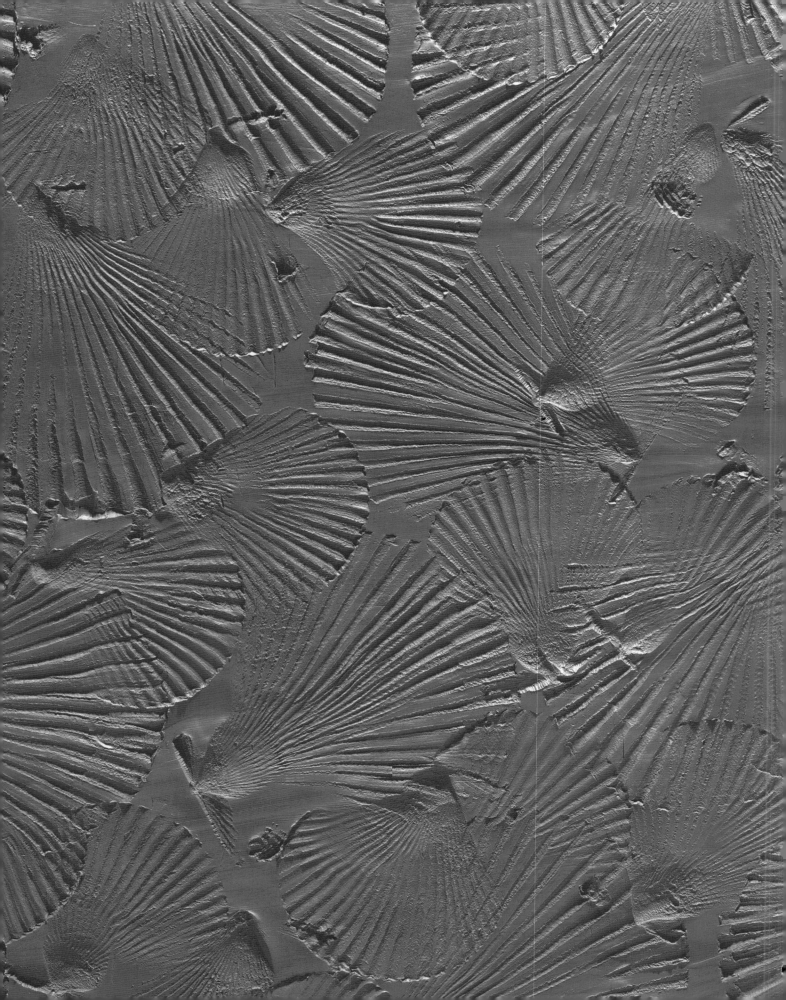

Matter and Energy

UNIT EXPERIMENT

Solids in Water

How does water temperature change the way solids dissolve? Plan and do a test to find out.

Investigate Matter

Vocabulary

matter
solid
liquid
float
sink
dissolve
gas
change

Did You Know?
Boats **float** higher in salt water than they do in fresh water.

Did You Know?
Some liquids **sink** in other liquids.

E3

What Can We Observe About Solids?

Investigate

Solid Objects

You will need

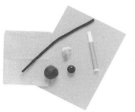

objects

paper and pencil

1 Observe each object.

2 Compare the sizes, shapes, and colors of the objects.

3 Think of three ways to classify the objects. Draw or write them on your paper.

Science Skill

To classify the objects, find ways they are the same and group them.

Matter and Solids

Everything around you is **matter**.
Toys and blocks are matter. You are, too!

■ **What matter do you see?**

Observing Solids

Some matter is solid. A **solid** is matter that keeps its shape. It keeps its shape even when you move it.

■ How do you know these toys are solids?

Sorting Solids

You can sort solids in many ways. You can sort toys by color. This graph shows how many toys of each color there are.

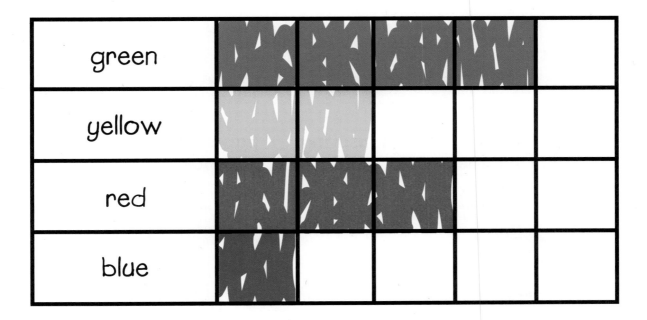

green					
yellow					
red					
blue					

- **What other ways could you sort the toys in the toy box?**

Think About It

1. What is matter?

2. What is a solid?

What Can We Observe About Liquids?

 **Investigate**

Liquids in Bottles

You will need

3 containers   **measuring cup**   **paper and pencil**

1 Draw the shape of the water in each container.

2 Which container do you think has the most water?

3 Measure the water. Write a number for each container. Use the numbers to tell what you found out.

Science Skill

You can write numbers when you measure. Use the numbers to compare the things you measured.

Liquids

Matter that flows is called a **liquid**. A liquid does not have a shape of its own. It takes the shape of the container you pour it into.

Observing Liquids

Some liquids, like water, are thin.
Others are thick.

■ **What liquids are thick?**

Some liquids mix with water. Vinegar mixes with water. Oil does not mix with water.

oil   vinegar

Think About It

1. What is a liquid?

2. What can we observe about liquids?

What Objects Sink or Float?

Shapes That Sink or Float

You will need

ball of clay

aquarium with water

paper and pencil

1 Gather data about shapes that sink or float. Put the clay ball in the water.

2 Record data about what happens.

3 Make the clay into different shapes. Do they sink or float? Record.

Science Skill

When you gather data, you observe things. When you record data, you write and draw what you observe.

Objects That Sink or Float

Some objects **float** , or stay on top of a liquid. Others **sink** , or drop to the bottom of a liquid. You can change the shape of some objects to make them float or sink.

Floaters and Sinkers

Some objects have shapes that help them float. Others have shapes that make them sink.

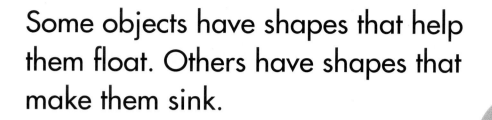

You can not always guess which objects will float. You must test them to find out.

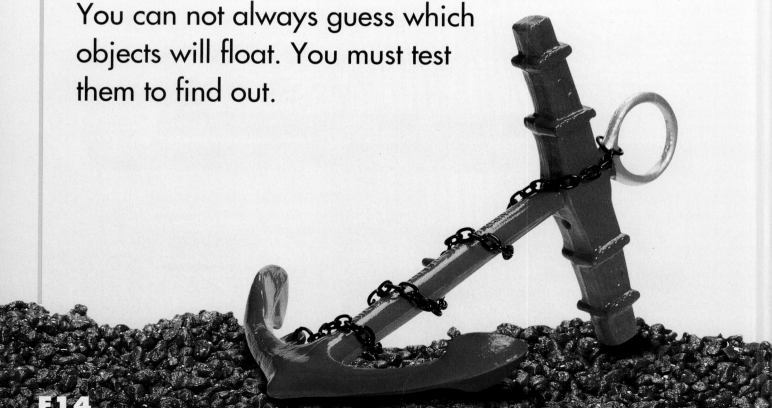

You can group objects as floaters or sinkers. What objects here would you put into these two groups? Why?

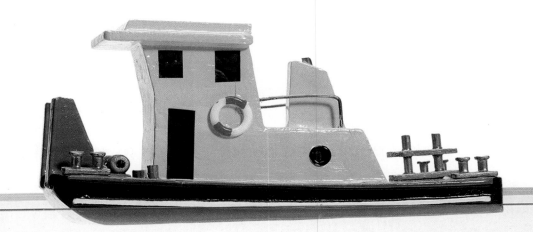

Think About It

1. What do *float* and *sink* mean?
2. What helps an object sink or float?

What Solids Dissolve in Liquids?

Solids in Water

You will need

stirring stick   paper and pencil   solids to test   4 cups of water

1 What do you think these solids will do in water? Form a hypothesis for each one.

2 Put a solid into water. Stir for a minute. When the water stops swirling, observe.

3 Can you see the solid in the water? Record what you observe. Repeat for the other solids.

Solids in Water				
	My hypothesis		My results	
	Will dissolve	Will not dissolve	Did dissolve	Did not dissolve
salt				
sand				
rocks				
baking soda				

Science Skill

When you form a hypothesis you choose and test a possible answer.

Solids in Liquids

Some solids do not mix well with a liquid. They do not **dissolve**, or mix with the liquid completely. Soil and sand do not dissolve in water.

soil in water

E17

Observing Solids That Dissolve

Some solids you use at home dissolve in water. Sugar and salt dissolve in water. Baking soda dissolves in water. Many kinds of drink mixes also dissolve in water.

drink mixes

Some solids dissolve faster in a hot liquid than in a cold liquid. Salt dissolves quickly in hot water but slowly in cold water.

■ **What happens when you put sugar into liquids at different temperatures?**

Think About It

1. What happens when a solid dissolves in a liquid?
2. When do some solids dissolve faster in a liquid?

What Can We Observe About Gases?

Air in a Bottle

You will need

balloon

plastic soft drink bottle

1 Squeeze the bottle to observe the air in it. Blow up the balloon. Feel the air come out.

2 Put the balloon in the bottle. Pull the end over the top.

3 Try to blow up the balloon. What else is in the bottle? Draw a conclusion.

Science Skill

To draw a conclusion about what happened, think about what you observed.

 **Learn About**

Gases

Gases are matter. A **gas** does not have a shape of its own. It spreads out to fill its container and take its shape.

How Can We Change Objects?

Changing Paper

You will need

4 cards with slits

paints and brushes

glitter

glue

paper and pencil

1 Observe the cards. Record how they look and feel.

2 How could you change the way the cards look and feel? Investigate your ideas.

3 Record how you change the cards.

> ### Science Skill
> To investigate, think of changes you could make, and then try them out.

Changing Objects

You can **change** objects, or make them different. You can change their shape, size, color, or texture.

Tell What You Know

1. Use the word *solid, liquid,* or *gas* to tell about each picture.

Vocabulary

Use each word to tell about the picture.

2.

matter

3.

float

4.

sink

5.
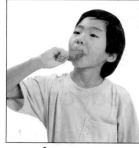

change

6.

dissolve

Using Science Skills

7. **Gather and Record Data**
Make a chart to gather and record data about liquids. Put one drop of water and one drop of oil on wax paper.

Liquids				
	Makes a Round Drop	Makes a Flat Drop	Can Be Dragged	Can Not Be Dragged
Water				
Oil				

Observe each drop. Use a toothpick to drag each one. Try other liquids and add them to the chart.

8. **Draw a Conclusion** Think about what makes these cars roll. Draw a conclusion about why one car rolled farther.

Making Sound

Vocabulary

sound
vibrate
pitch
musical
instrument

Did You Know?
This organ is the
world's largest
musical instrument.
It is inside a cave.

Did You Know? Rabbits hear **sound** with their long ears. Sounds may warn them of danger.

What Are Sounds?

Investigate

Sounds

You will need

cardboard
tube

ruler

pencil

foil

rubber
band

1 Hum into the cardboard tube. Listen to the sound.

2 Punch a hole that is 2 centimeters from one end of the tube. Use the rubber band to hold foil over the other end.

3 Hum and listen again. Now investigate this problem. How can you change the foil or the tube to change the humming sound?

Science Skill

To investigate a problem, you test different ideas.

 **Learn About**

Sound

Everything you hear is **sound**. You might hear the beating of a drum. You might hear the call of an elephant. You might also hear the voice of a friend. Sound is all around you.

How Sounds Are Made

If you pluck a stretched rubber band, you may hear a sound. You may also see the rubber band move back and forth very fast. To move back and forth very fast is to **vibrate**.

When the rubber band stops vibrating, the sound stops.

Sound is made when things vibrate. A ball vibrates inside a whistle. You can feel it vibrate.

Gently touch your throat while you hum. Then stop humming. Something in your throat vibrates and then stops. Tell what it feels like.

Sounds You Hear

You can hear the sound of your own voice. You can whisper and shout. You can laugh and cry. You can cover your mouth to make your voice quiet. You can cup your hands around your mouth to make your voice loud.

microphone

megaphone

■ What are these people using to change the sound of their voices?

Some sounds are nice to hear, like the sound of waves crashing against rocks. Other sounds, like sirens blowing, are not so nice. The more carefully you listen, the more sounds you can hear.

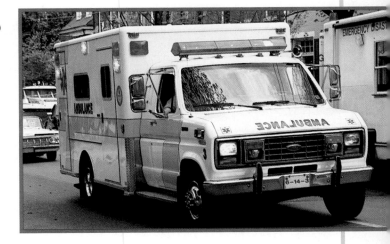

Think About It

1. How are sounds made?
2. What happens when something stops vibrating?

How Are Sounds Different?

Some Different Sounds

You will need

4 bottles **labels** **water** **measuring cup**

1 Make labels. Put each one in front of a bottle.

2 Measure and pour the right amount of water into each bottle.

3 Blow across the top of each bottle. Tell about the sounds you make. Use numbers to tell about the bottles for the different sounds.

Science Skill

You can use numbers to tell how the amount of water changes sound.

E40

Different Sounds

There are many kinds of sounds. A big train makes a loud, low sound. A small train makes a higher, quieter sound. You may be able to infer how big a train is just by listening to its sound.

Quiet and Loud Sounds

Some sounds are quiet, and some sounds are loud. A small stream makes a quiet sound. A big waterfall makes a loud sound.

A kitten often makes a quiet sound. A tiger often makes a loud sound.

Some things can make both loud sounds and quiet sounds. When you shout, your voice makes a loud sound. When you whisper, you make a quiet sound.

Drums can make loud and quiet sounds, too. When a drummer hits a drum hard, it makes a loud sound. With gentle taps, the drum makes a quiet sound.

High and Low Sounds

Some sounds are high, and some sounds are low. The **pitch** of a sound is how high or low the sound is. A big dog's bark has a low pitch. A big bell has a low pitch, too. A man's voice also has a low pitch.

The bark of a small dog and ringing chimes have high pitches. A boy's voice has high pitch, too.

Think About It

1. How is the sound of a kitten different from the sound of a tiger?
2. What is the pitch of a sound?

What Sounds Do Instruments Make?

 Investigate

Making Your Own Drum

You will need

 a small can

 beans

 balloon

 rubber band

 pencil with eraser

1 Put the beans into the can. Stretch the balloon over the top. Put the rubber band on.

2 Form a hypothesis about your drum. What kind of sound will it make? What will vibrate?

3 Test your hypothesis. Use the pencil to beat the drum. Listen for the sounds.

Science Skill

When you form a hypothesis, you choose and test a possible answer.

Instrument Sounds

The boys and girls are making music together. Each person is playing a **musical instrument**, something used to make music. Each instrument has its own sound.

Listen to Instrument Sounds

A musical instrument makes sound when part of it vibrates. Some instruments have parts that vibrate very fast. These instruments make a sound with a high pitch. Other instruments have parts that vibrate more slowly. These make a sound with a low pitch.

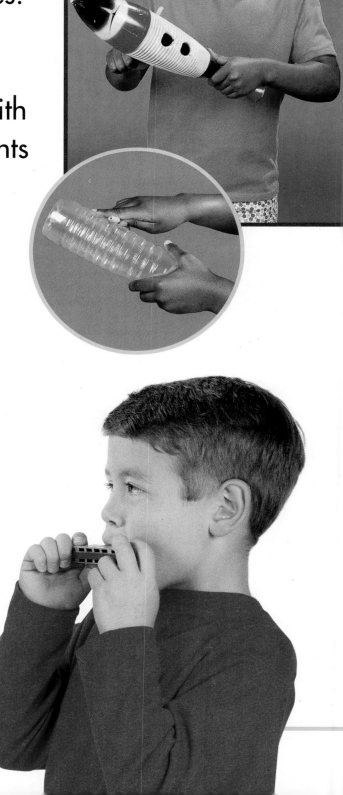

Instruments are played in different ways. A drummer beats a drum to make its covering vibrate. Players sometimes pluck the strings of an instrument to make them vibrate.

Think About It

1. In what way are all musical instruments the same?
2. How are musical instruments different?

 Social Studies Link

Sounds from Around the World

People all over the world use musical instruments to make sounds. These instruments make sounds when you hit them. They are used to make a beat.

Write

You can use your hands as a musical instrument. Clap to make a beat. Then change the beat. Listen to the sounds you make. Pots and pans can make sounds like instruments, too. Write about which of these sounds you like better.

Math Link

Measure How Far a Whisper Travels

A whisper is a quiet sound. It can not be heard from far away. You can measure how far a whisper travels.

Think and Do

Make a long tape line on the floor. Measure and mark every meter with an **X**. Stand one meter from a classmate. Can you hear a whisper? Move farther away, one meter at a time. Find out how far the sound of a whisper travels.

Tell What You Know

1. Tell what you know about each musical instrument.

Vocabulary

Use each word to tell about the picture.

2.
vibrate

3.
sound

4.
pitch

Using Science Skills

5. **Use Numbers** Make four shakers by putting dried beans inside plastic cups taped together. The numbers in the chart tell how many dried beans to put in each shaker. How does the number of dried beans change the sound a shaker makes? Record your ideas.

Number of Dried Beans	2	10	20	40
Sound the Shaker Makes				

6. **Form a Hypothesis** Hold a bell by the handle at the top. Use a spoon to strike the side of the bell. Listen for the sound. Then hold the bell by the side. Form a hypothesis about the sound the bell will make now. Test your hypothesis.

Activities
for Home or School

Make Juice Bars

Change liquid juice into a solid by making juice bars.

1. Have a family member help you pour fruit juice into an ice cube tray.

2. Put a toothpick into each part of the tray. *Be careful. Toothpicks are sharp.*

3. Freeze and eat!

Floating Drops

1. Fill a jar with salad oil.

2. Put two or three drops of food coloring into the oil. Put the lid on the jar.

3. Tip the jar. What happens to the colored drops? Talk about what floats and why.

Listen for Sounds

1. Close your eyes and sit quietly for one minute. Do not speak or move.

2. Listen carefully for sounds.

3. Draw pictures to show the sounds you heard.

4. Compare with a classmate or family member. Which sounds did both of you hear?

Find the Sound

1. All players close their eyes.

2. One player is "it" and rings a bell softly.

3. The other players guess where the sound is coming from.

4. The player who locates "it" makes the next sound.

Georgia Rural Telephone Museum, Leslie, Georgia

At this museum, you can learn about the telephone. You can learn how sound travels long distances. You can also see how the telephone has changed over time.

Plan Your Own Expedition

Visit a museum near you. Or log on to The Learning Site.

GO ONLINE www.harcourtschool.com

Forces

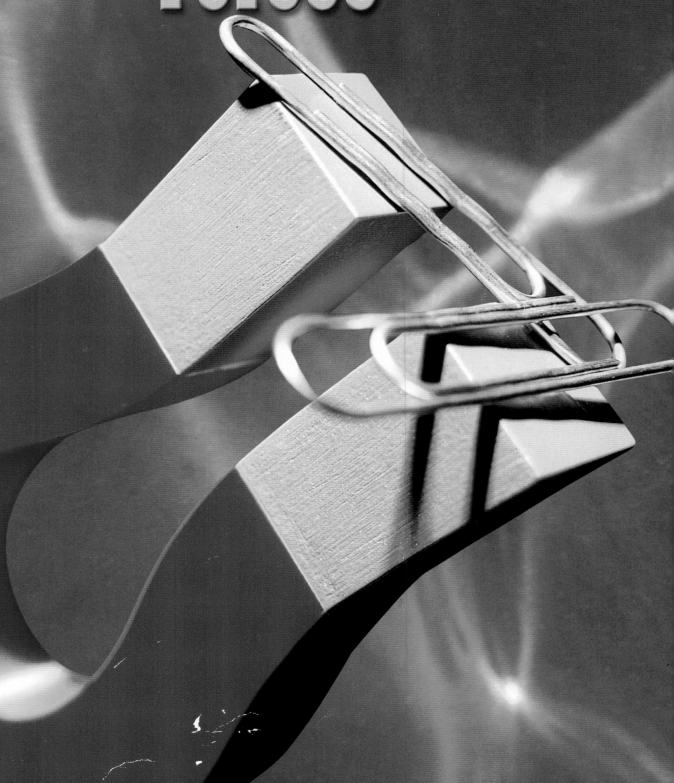

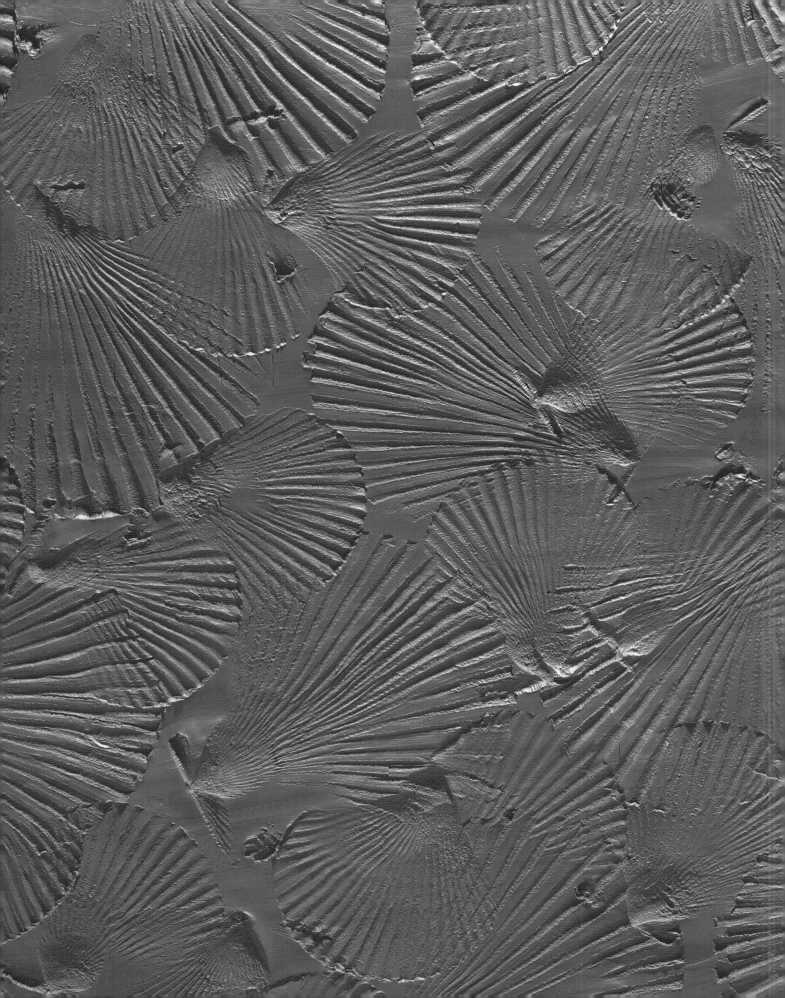

Forces

UNIT EXPERIMENT

Height and Distance

How will the height of a ramp change the distance a car travels? Plan and do a test to find out.

Vocabulary

force
push
pull
curve
motion
speed
surface
friction
wheel

Did You Know?
Tree roots can **push** a rock when they grow.

Did You Know?
The golden wheel spider can roll like a **wheel**.

What Makes Things Move?

Pushes and Pulls

You will need

small block

things to make the block move

paper and pencil

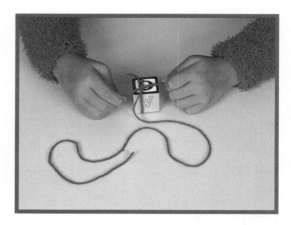

1 What could you do to push or pull the block?

2 Write a plan to investigate your ideas. Then follow your plan.

3 Tell what you used to move the block. Use the word *push* or *pull*.

Science Skill
You **investigate** by thinking of ideas and trying them out.

Making Things Move

A **force** is a push or a pull. When you **push** something, you press it away. When you **pull** something, you tug it closer.

push

pull

Pushes and Pulls

Pushes and pulls make things move or stop moving. A tow truck pulls a car to the repair shop. A player pushes with a glove to stop a moving ball.

■ Would the player use a push or a pull to throw the ball?

A push or a pull can make something change direction. When you kick a ball, you are using a push. First the ball rolls to you. Your push makes it change direction. Then it moves away from you.

■ **What will the ball do when the player kicks it?**

Think About It

1. What is a force?

2. What can pushes and pulls do?

What Are Some Ways Things Move?

 Investigate

Moving Objects

You will need

objects

paper and pencil

1 Observe and record how each object moves when you push or pull it.

2 Group objects that move the same way. Write how you grouped them.

Science Skill

To group the objects, put those that move in the same way together.

Ways Things Move

Pushes and pulls make things move in different ways. Tell what you know about how these rides move.

Telling How Things Move

There are different ways to tell how things move. One way is by the path they make. A train moves in a straight path. It may **curve**, or bend, along its path.

straight

curve

There is another way to tell how things move. Two bikers may start at the same time. If one moves ahead, he or she is moving faster.

Some things move the same way over and over. A top spins round and round. A swing moves back and forth.

■ **What kind of force keeps a swing moving?**

Think About It

1. What are some ways things move?
2. How can you tell if one thing is moving faster than another?

Why Do Things Move the Way They Do?

 Investigate

Predicting Motion

You will need

ramp

plastic ball

tape

block

1 Set up the ramp. Predict where the ball will stop. Mark that place with tape.

2 Let the ball roll down the ramp. Was your prediction right?

3 Now put the block where the ball will hit it. Do Step 2 again.

Science Skill

To predict where the ball will stop, think about how a ball rolls and bounces.

Why Things Move the Way They Do

Moving from one place to another is **motion**. You can observe the motion of an object. This will help you predict where it will move next.

Changing Motion

A push or pull can change the motion of something. A hockey puck moves straight ahead unless something changes its motion.

Different kinds of pushes change the **speed**, how quickly or slowly the puck moves. A hard push moves the puck quickly. A gentle push moves it slowly.

■ **What kind of push should the player use to move the puck slowly?**

Changing Direction

A force can change the direction in which an object moves. A ball will roll in one direction until something pushes it and makes it change.

■ What does the paddle do to the ball in table tennis?

Bumps are the pushes that change the direction of bumper boats. When you bump your boat against another boat, your boat bounces back.

Think About It

1. What is motion?
2. What can change the motion of something?

How Do Objects Move on Surfaces?

Smooth and Rough Surfaces

You will need

ramp

toy truck

meterstick

paper and pencil

1 Set up a ramp on a smooth surface. Let the truck roll down.

2 Measure how far it rolls. Record the number. Do the same on a rough surface.

3 On which surface does the truck roll farther? Use your numbers to tell.

Science Skill

Measure how far the truck rolls from the end of the ramp to where the truck stops.

Different Surfaces

A **surface** is the top or outside of something. This floor has both a smooth surface and a rough surface. The truck moves in a different way on each surface.

More Friction, Less Friction

When two surfaces rub together, they make friction. **Friction** is a force that makes it harder to move things.

A rough surface makes more friction than a smooth one. On a rough road, a bike is harder to move. You have to push harder on the pedals.

■ **What surfaces rub together when you ride a bike over a road?**

You can change how much friction a surface makes. If you cover a surface with something wet, it makes less friction. If you cover a surface with something rough, it makes more friction.

Think About It

1. What is friction?

2. What kind of surface makes more friction? What kind makes less friction?

How Do Wheels Help Objects Move?

 Investigate

Rollers

You will need

rollers

heavy book

toy truck

tape

1 Push the book. Then put rollers under it. Push again. Which is easier?

2 Push the truck. Tape the wheels, and push it again. Which is easier?

3 Draw a conclusion about wheels and rollers.

> **Science Skill**
> To draw a conclusion about something, use what you have observed to explain what happens.

What Wheels Can Do

A roller is any object that rolls. A **wheel** is a roller that turns on an axle. Rollers and wheels make things easier to push or pull.

Many Ways to Use Wheels

People use wheels in many ways. They use baskets on wheels to carry things when they shop. They use chairs on wheels to help them move around. Some children put wheels on boxes to make play cars.

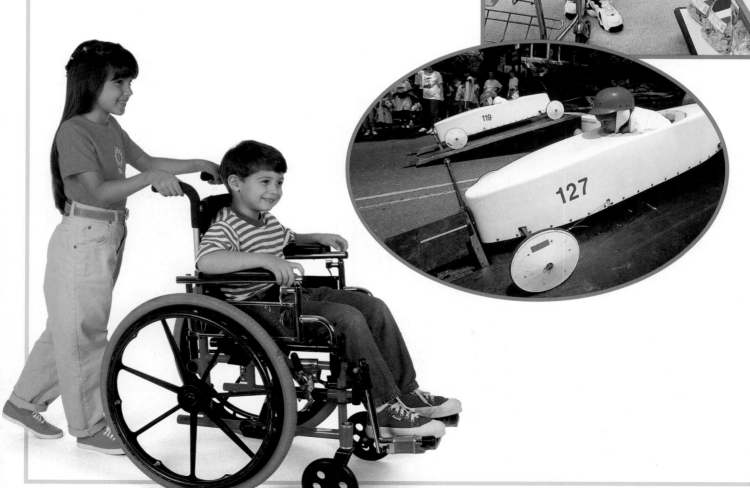

People use wheels to help them push or pull loads. A dolly's wheels make it easy to push heavy boxes. Many suitcases have wheels so that people can pull them along.

■ **Why do people use things that have wheels?**

Think About It

1. What is a wheel?
2. What can wheels do?

An Architect Plans Buildings

I. M. Pei designs buildings. He knows about forces that push and pull. He designs buildings that won't fall down.

Think and Do

Use index cards to build a house. Then blow on your house of cards. Find different ways to make a house you can not blow down.

Math Link

Add Pushes for Points

In some games, players use pushes to score points. Air hockey and bowling are two games like this.

Write

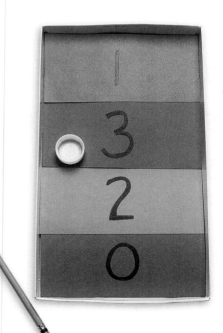

Make a game that uses pushes to score points. Use a box lid. Then use a pencil to flip a bottle cap ten times into the lid.

Add the number it lands on to your score each time. Then write about the kind of push you use to get the most points.

Tell What You Know

1. Tell what you know about the picture. Use the words *force*, *motion*, *surface*, and *friction*.

Vocabulary

Tell which picture goes best with each word.

2. push
3. pull
4. curve
5. speed
6. wheel

a.

b.

c.

d.

e.

Using Science Skills

7. **Measure** Pull a rock across rough and smooth surfaces with a rubber band. Measure how long the rubber band stretches each time. Make a chart. Record the numbers. Which makes more friction?

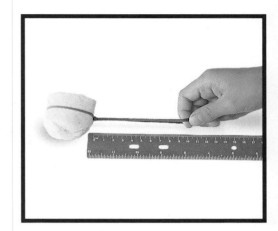

Friction on Surfaces	
Surface	How Long the Rubber Band Stretches
rough	
smooth	

8. **Draw a Conclusion** Rub your hands together. Feel the friction. Then put a few drops of oil on your hands. Rub again. Draw a conclusion.

CHAPTER 2

Magnets

Vocabulary

magnet
attract
strength
poles
repel
magnetic force
magnetize

Did You Know?
The Maglev train uses **magnets** to move.

Did You Know?
These magnets can **repel** each other.

What Are Magnets?

 Investigate

What a Magnet Can Do

You will need

bar magnet   objects   paper and pencil

What a Magnet Can Do		
Object	Pulls	Does Not Pull

1 Gather data about the magnet. Hold it near each object.

2 Make a chart like this one. Record what you observe.

3 Group the objects the magnet pulls and those it does not pull.

Science Skill

To gather data about what a magnet can do, observe and record what it does.

Magnets

A **magnet** is a piece of iron that can **attract**, or pull, things. The things it pulls are usually made of iron. Iron is a kind of metal.

■ How are magnets used here?

How People Use Magnets

People use magnets to hold things closed and to lift things. They also use them in televisions and electric motors.

A farmer may put a magnet in a cow's stomach. The magnet attracts bits of metal that the cow may eat. This keeps the metal from hurting the cow.

cow magnet

Where Magnets Can Be Found

Some magnets are found in nature. Lodestone is a kind of magnet found in the ground.

lodestone

■ How are the children using magnets in this fishing game?

How Magnets Are the Same and Different

Magnets are the same in one way. They attract objects made of iron. They do not attract objects made of other materials.

Magnets may be different in other ways. They may be round or square, big or small, straight or curved. They may be different colors.

Magnets may be different in **strength**, or how strongly they pull. One magnet may attract more paper clips than another.

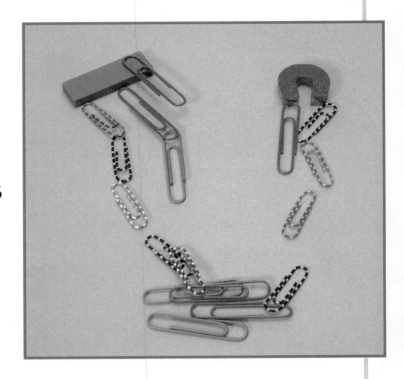

■ **Look at the chart. Which magnet has the greater strength?**

Magnet Strength	
Magnet	Number of Clips
bar magnet	6
horseshoe magnet	3

Think About It

1. What is a magnet?
2. What are some ways people use magnets?

What Are the Poles of a Magnet?

Investigate

A Magnet's Ends

You will need

bar magnet   paper clips   paper and pencil

1 Pick up paper clips with one end of the magnet. Record the number. Then do the other end.

2 Pick up paper clips with the middle of the magnet. Record the number.

3 Make a bar graph. Infer which parts of the magnet are strongest.

Science Skill

To infer which parts of the magnet are the strongest, compare the numbers in your bar graph.

The Poles of a Magnet

A magnet has two **poles**. These are the places where its pulling force is strongest. Where are the poles of this bar magnet? How can you tell?

What Poles Can Do

Every magnet has a north pole and a south pole. They are often called the *N* pole and the *S* pole.

Two poles that are different attract each other. An *N* pole and an *S* pole attract each other.

Two poles that are the same **repel**, or push each other away. Two *N* poles repel each other.

■ **What do you think two S poles would do?**

Bits of iron can show where a magnet's pull is strongest. The iron bits make a pattern around the magnet. More bits go to the poles, where the pull is strongest.

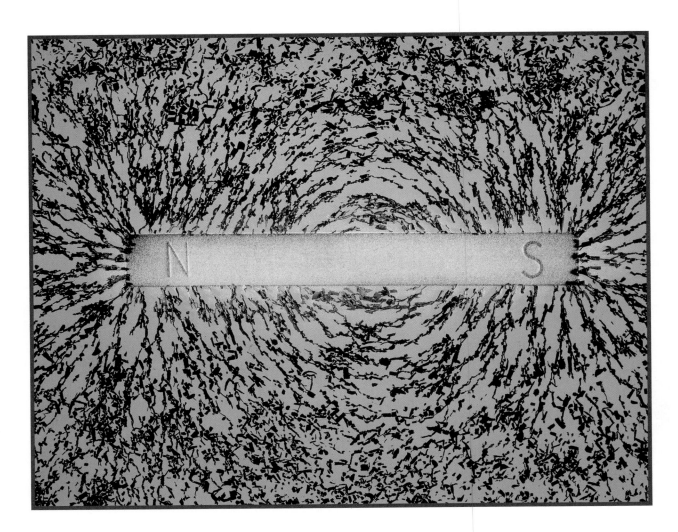

Think About It

1. What are poles?

2. What do poles do?

What Can a Magnet Pull Through?

Things Magnets Pull Through

You will need

bar magnet

paper clips

different materials

1 Can a magnet attract paper clips through things? Plan an investigation to find out. Write your plan.

2 Follow your plan to investigate your ideas. Record what you observe.

3 Use your data to communicate what you find out.

Science Skill

To investigate what things a magnet can pull through, first make a plan and then try your ideas.

The Force of a Magnet

A magnet's pull is called **magnetic force**. This force can pass through some things to attract iron objects.

■ **What material is magnetic force passing through to attract these puppets?**

Observing Magnetic Force

The magnetic force of a magnet can pass through paper or cloth. It can also pass through water and glass.

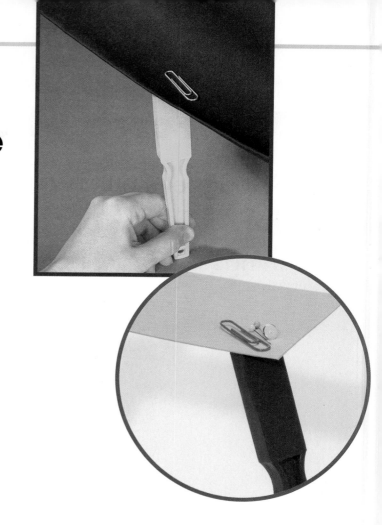

- **What do you think might happen if the glass were thicker?**

Magnetic force is strong close to a magnet. It can pull a paper clip through the air. Farther away, it may not be strong enough to do this.

Think About It

1. What is magnetic force?
2. What are some materials magnetic force can pass through?

How Can You Make a Magnet?

Making a Magnet

You will need

magnet

2 paper clips

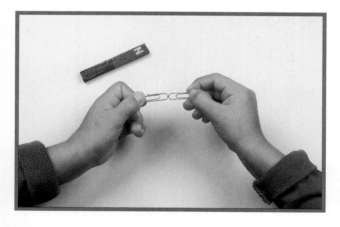

1 Touch one clip to the other. Observe.

2 Use the magnet to pick up one clip. Touch that clip to the other one. Observe.

3 Take away the magnet. Draw a conclusion. How can you make a magnet?

Science Skill

To draw a conclusion, use what you have observed to form an idea.

Making a Magnet

A magnet can **magnetize**, or give magnetic force to, things it attracts. The magnet on this crane has magnetized some pieces of metal. Their new magnetic force attracts more pieces.

Ways to Make a Magnet

You can magnetize an iron nail. Stroke the nail on the magnet ten times the same way. Then the nail will be magnetized for a short time.

■ How can you tell that this nail is now a magnet?

Some magnets are made from iron heated with other materials. These magnets are made in a factory.

Magnet Engineer

A magnet engineer finds new ways to make magnets. These magnets may be stronger or last longer than iron ones.

Think About It

1. What can you use to magnetize an object made of iron?
2. How can you make a magnet?

Math Link

Measure Magnetic Force

You can compare the strengths of different magnets. To do this, you will need to record how far their magnetic forces reach.

Write

Lay a paper clip at one end of a paper strip. Hold one magnet at the other end. Slide the magnet slowly toward the clip. Mark where the magnet is when the clip moves.

Do the same thing with each magnet. Write about the strength of each magnet.

Compass Readings

Long ago, travelers used compasses to find their way. Travelers still use them today. A compass has a magnetized needle that always points north.

Think and Do

Make your own compass. Float a plastic plate in water. Place a bar magnet in the center of the plate. Turn the plate. Which way is north?

Tell What You Know

1. Use the words *strength*, *poles*, and *magnetic force* to tell about each picture.

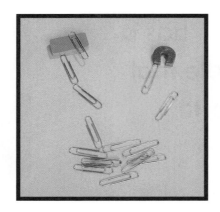

Vocabulary

Tell which picture goes with each word.

2. magnet

3. attract

4. repel

5. magnetize

a.

b.

c.

d.

Using Science Skills

6. Infer Look at the two patterns made by the bits of iron. Which magnet made each pattern? How do you know?

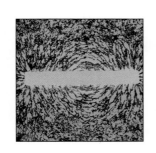

7. Investigate Some people use a metal detector to help them find things made of metal.

Play a metal detector game. Ask a partner to put three metal objects in a group of objects.

Predict which objects your magnet will attract. Investigate to find out.

Activities
for Home or School

Magnetic Kite

1. Cut out a tissue paper kite.
2. Attach thread and a paper clip.
3. Tape the thread's tail to a table.
4. Use the magnet to pick up your kite without touching it.

Magnetic Race-Car Game

1. Draw a road on cardboard.
2. Put two paper clips on the road.
3. Put two magnets under the cardboard. Move the magnets to race your clips.

Make a Water Wheel

1. Push toothpicks into the ends of a piece of clay. *Be careful. Toothpicks are sharp.*

2. Push strips cut from a carton into the clay to make a water wheel.

3. Hold the wheel by the toothpicks. Place the wheel under running water.

4. Tell how the water makes the wheel turn.

Marble Fun Slide

1. Tape together paper towel tubes to make a fun slide.

2. Use books to hold up the tubes.

3. Put a marble at the top, and listen to it race to the bottom. Talk about how it moves.

PLACES TO VISIT

Brookhaven National Laboratory Science Museum, Long Island, New York

At this science museum, you can learn about magnets. You can predict, classify, and test the ways magnets work.

Plan Your Own Expedition

Visit a museum or science center near you. Or log on to The Learning Site.

GO ONLINE   www.harcourtschool.com

References

Science Handbook

Using Science Tools

Hand Lens

1. Hold the hand lens close to your face.
2. Move the object until you see it clearly.

Thermometer

The temperature is 40 degrees.

1. Place the thermometer.
2. Wait two minutes.
3. Find the top of the liquid in the tube.
4. Read the number.

Ruler

1. Put the edge of the ruler at the end of the object.

2. Look at the number at the other end.

3. Read how long the object is.

This leaf is 21 cm long.

Measuring Cup

1. Pour the liquid into the cup.
2. Put the cup on a table.
3. Wait until the liquid is still.
4. Look at the level of the liquid.
5. Read how much liquid there is.

There are 150 milliliters of liquid here.

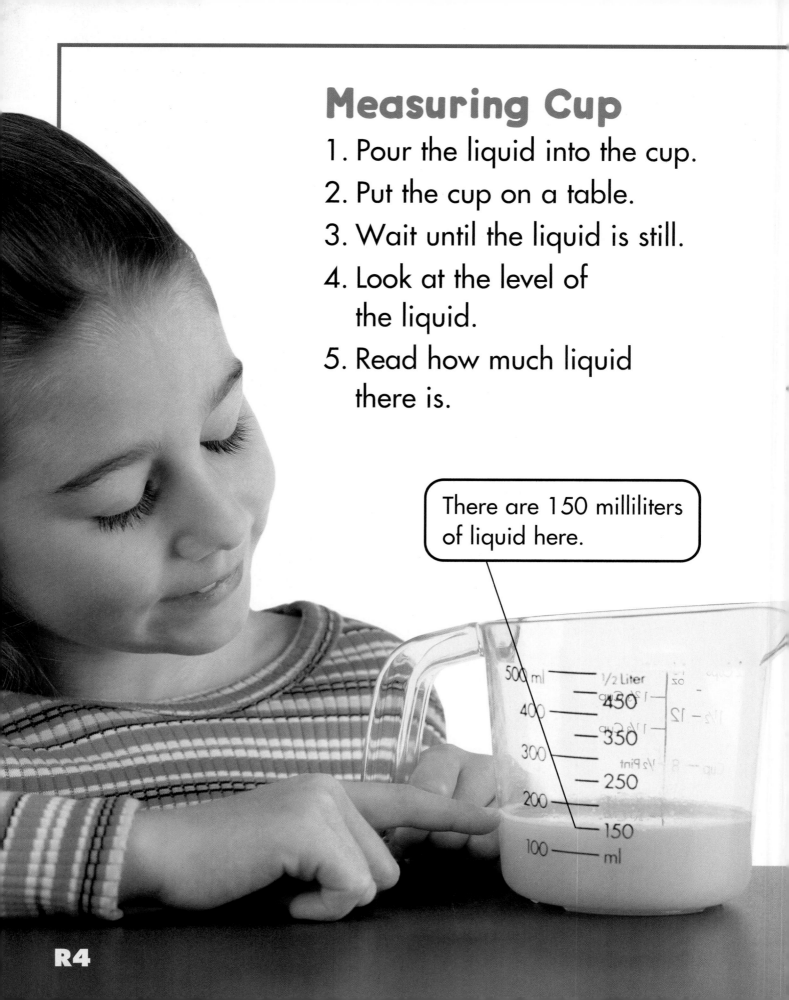

It is 10:00.

Clock

1. Look at the hour hand.
2. Look at the minute hand.
3. Read the time.

Stopwatch

1. To start timing, press START.
2. To stop timing, press STOP.
3. Read how much time has passed.

Now 15 seconds have gone by.

Balance

1. Start with the pans even.
2. Put the object in one pan.
3. Add masses until the pans are even again.
4. Count up the number of masses.

Magnet

1. Put one of the poles of the magnet near the object.

2. Look at the object to see if the magnet attracts it.

3. Make sure that you don't drop or hit the magnet.

4. Make sure that you don't put the magnet near a computer or other objects that have a magnet inside.

5. Store the magnet by placing a piece of steel or another magnet on the poles.

Measurements

1 cm

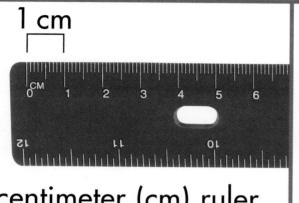

centimeter (cm) ruler

1 in.

inch (in.) ruler

Water freezes at 32°F. — Water freezes at 0°C.

Fahrenheit (F)
temperature

Celsius (C)
temperature

1 kilogram (kg)

1 pound (lb)

1 liter (L)

1 cup (c)

Health Handbook

Eyes and Ears

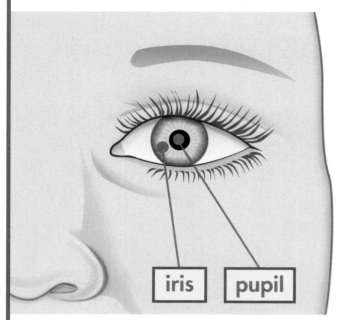

Outside of Eye

Caring for Your Eyes and Ears

- Some bright light can hurt your eyes. Never look at the sun or at very bright lights.
- Never put an object in your ear.

Eyes

When you look at your eyes, you can see a white part, a colored part, and a dark center. The colored part is the iris. The dark center is the pupil.

Inside of Eye

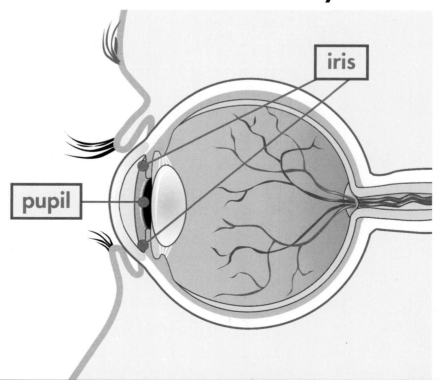

Ear

Your ears let you hear. Most of each ear is inside your head.

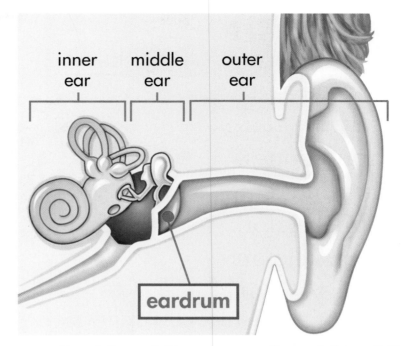

inner ear · middle ear · outer ear

eardrum

Inside of Ear   **Outside of Ear**

ACTIVITIES

1. The iris of the eye may be different colors. Look at the eyes of your classmates. How many colors do you see?

2. Ask a classmate to stand across the classroom from you. Have him or her say your name in a normal voice. Now put a hand behind each ear and have him or her say your name again in the same voice. Which time sounded louder?

The Skeletal System

Inside your body are hard, strong bones. They make up your skeleton. Your skeleton holds you up.

Caring for Your Skeletal System

Protect your head. Wear a helmet when you ride your bike.

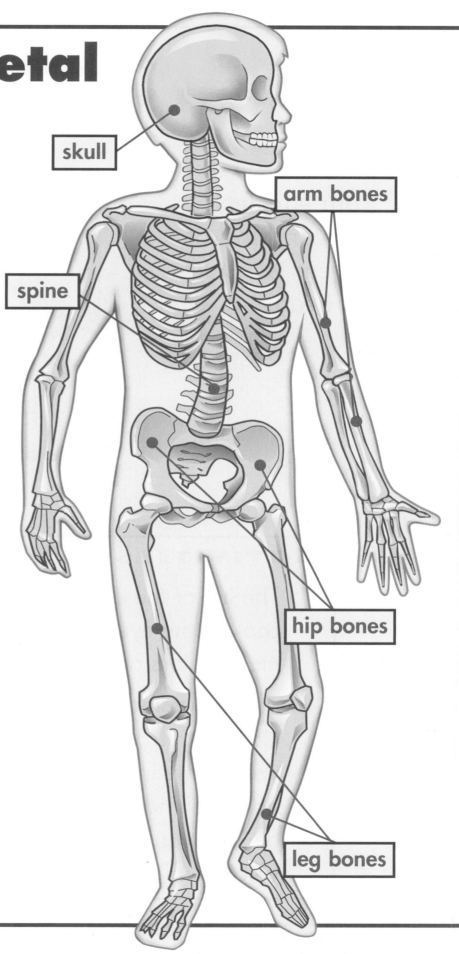

skull

arm bones

spine

hip bones

leg bones

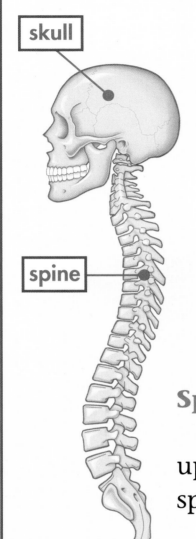

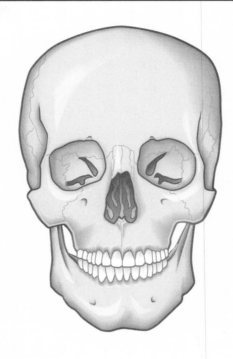

skull

spine

Skull

The bones in your head are called your skull. Your skull protects your brain.

Spine

Your spine, or backbone, is made up of many small bones. Your spine helps you stand up straight.

ACTIVITIES

1. Look at a bike helmet. How is it like your skull?

2. Your foot is about the same length as your arm between your hand and your elbow. Put your foot on your arm and check it out!

The Digestive System

Your digestive system helps your body get energy from the food you eat.

Caring for Your Digestive System

- Brush and floss your teeth every day.
- Don't eat right before you exercise. Your body needs energy to digest food.

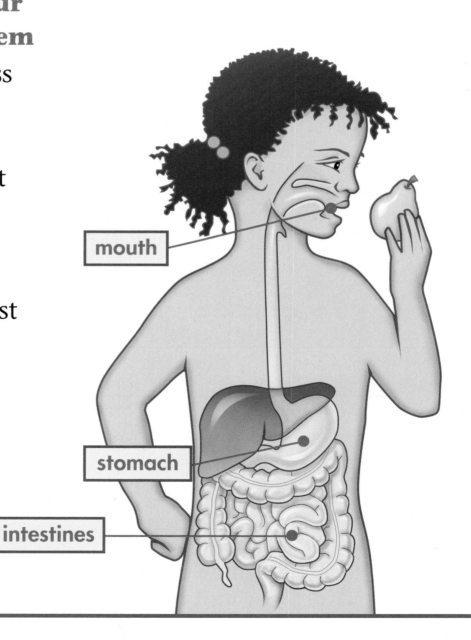

mouth

stomach

intestines

Teeth

Some of your teeth tear food and some grind it into small parts.

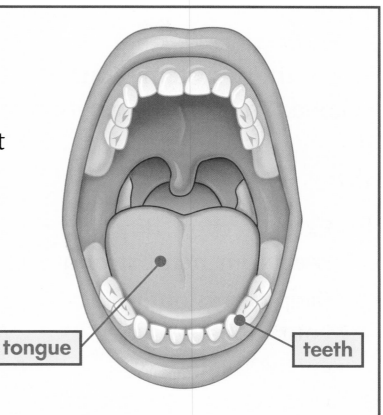

tongue

teeth

Tongue

Your tongue helps you swallow food. It is a strong muscle that also lets you taste.

ACTIVITIES

1. Bite into an apple and chew the bite. Which teeth did you use for these jobs?

2. Lick a salty pretzel and a lollipop. Compare how they taste.

The Circulatory System

Blood goes through your body in your circulatory system. Your heart pumps the blood. Your blood vessels carry the blood.

Caring for Your Circulatory System

- Exercise every day to keep your heart strong.
- Keep germs out of your blood. Wash cuts with soap and water. Never touch someone else's blood.

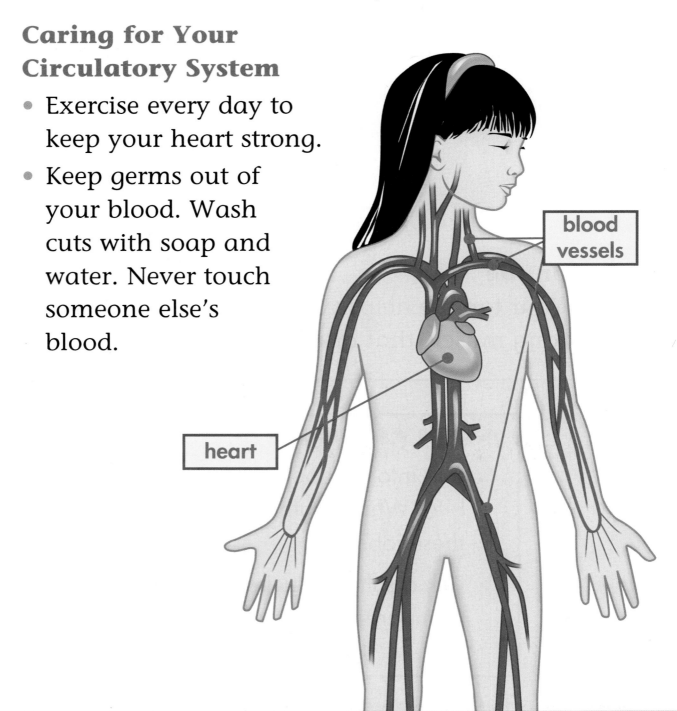

blood vessels

heart

Heart

Your heartbeat is the sound of your heart pumping. Your heart is about the same size as a fist.

fist

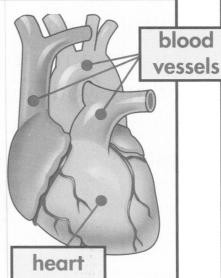

blood vessels

heart

Blood Vessels

Blood vessels are tubes that carry blood through your body.

ACTIVITIES

1. Ask an adult to blow up a hot-dog shaped balloon so that it is not quite full. Squeeze one end. What happens?

2. Put your ear to the middle of a classmate's chest and listen to the heartbeat. Then listen again through a paper cup with the bottom torn out. Which way of listening works better?

The Respiratory System

When you breathe, you are using your respiratory system. Your mouth, your nose, and your lungs are parts of your respiratory system.

Caring for Your Respiratory System

- Never put anything in your nose.
- Exercise makes you breathe harder and is good for your lungs.

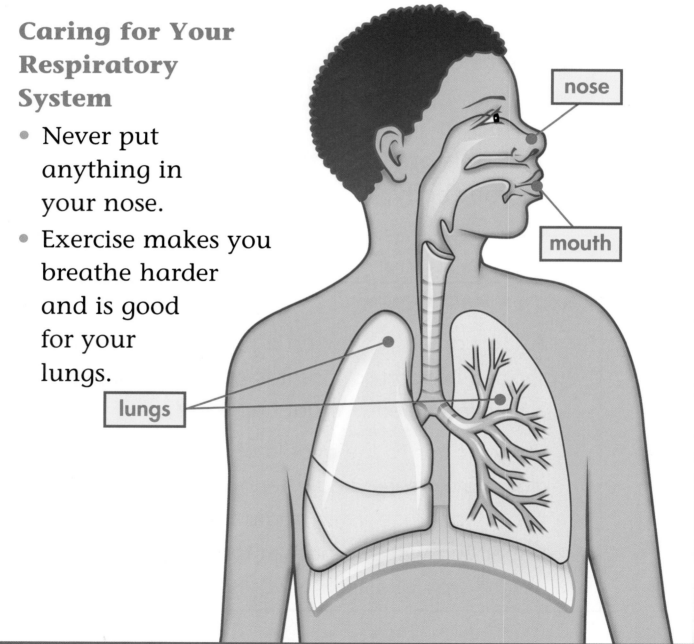

nose

mouth

lungs

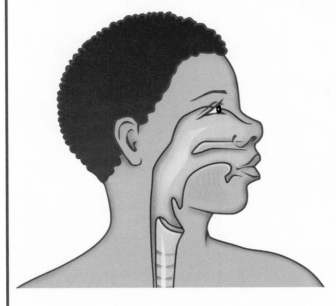

Mouth and Nose

Air goes in and out of your body through your mouth and nose.

Lungs

You have two lungs in your chest. When you breathe in, your lungs fill with air. When you breathe out, air leaves your lungs.

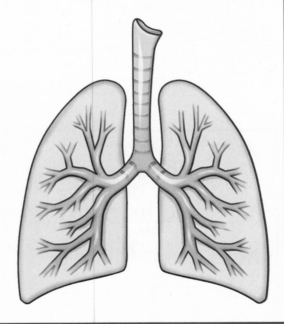

ACTIVITIES

1. Watch your chest and stomach muscles as you take a breath and let it out. Describe what happens.

2. Count how many breaths you take in one minute.

The Muscular System

The muscles in your body help you move.

Caring for Your Muscular System

Warm up your muscles before you play or exercise.

ACTIVITY

Hold your arm straight out from your body and lift it over your head. Then try it again with a book in your hand. How do the muscles in your arm feel?

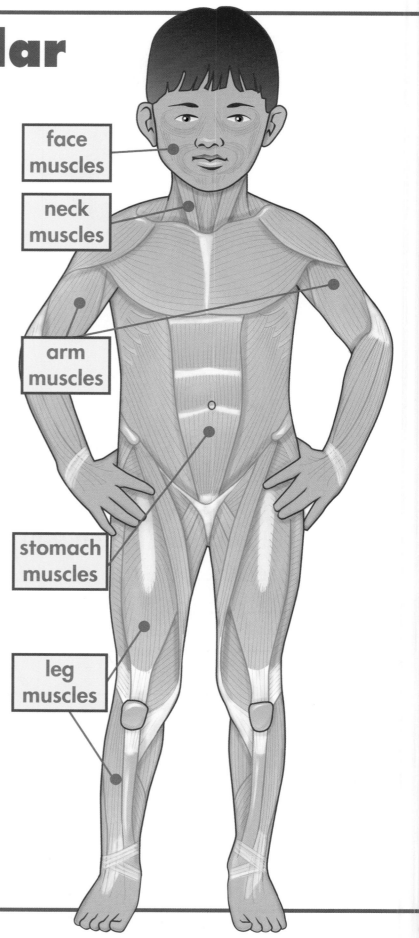

face muscles

neck muscles

arm muscles

stomach muscles

leg muscles

The Nervous System

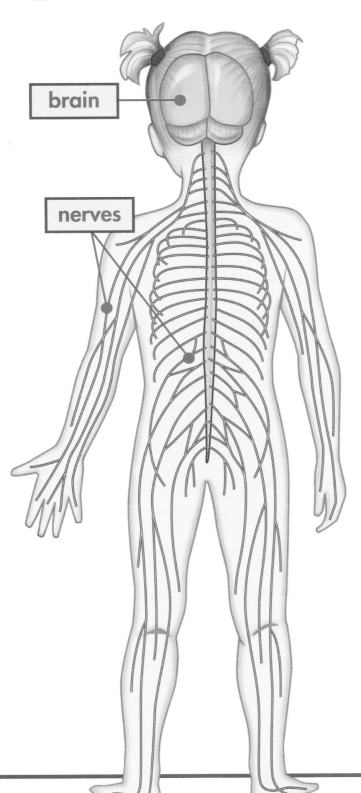

brain

nerves

Your nervous system keeps your body working and tells you about things around you. Your brain is part of your nervous system.

Caring for Your Nervous System

Get plenty of sleep. Sleeping lets your brain rest.

ACTIVITY

Clap your hands in front of a classmate's face. What happens to his or her eyes?

Staying Safe

Fire Safety

You can stay safe from fires. Follow these safety rules.

- Never play with matches or lighters.
- Be careful around stoves, heaters, fireplaces, and grills.
- Don't use microwaves, irons, or toasters without an adult's help.
- Practice your family's fire safety plan.
- If there is a fire in your home, get out quickly. Drop to the floor and crawl if the room is filled with smoke. If a closed door feels hot, don't open it. Use another exit. Call 911 from outside your home.
- If your clothes catch on fire, use Stop, Drop, and Roll right away to put out the flames.

1 Stop Don't run or wave your arms.

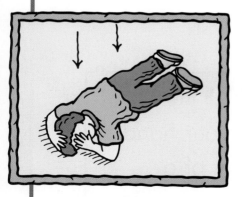

2 Drop Lie down quickly. Cover your eyes with your hands.

3 Roll Roll back and forth to put out the fire.

NO!

❶ Say no! Yell if you need to. You do not have to be polite to strangers.

Stranger Danger

You can stay safe around strangers. Follow these rules.

- Never talk to strangers.
- Never go with a stranger, on foot or in a car.
- If you are home alone, do not open the door. Do not let telephone callers know you are alone.
- Never give your name, address, or phone number to anyone you don't know. (You may give this information to a 911 operator in an emergency.)
- If you are lost or need help, talk to a police officer, a guard, or a store clerk.
- If a stranger bothers you, use the Stranger Danger rules to stay safe.

❷ Get away. Walk fast or run in the opposite direction. Go toward people who can help you.

❸ Tell someone. Tell a trusted adult, such as a family member, a teacher, or a police officer. Do not keep secrets about strangers.

R23

Staying Safe

A Safe Bike

To ride your bike safely, you need to start with a safe bike. A safe bike is the right size for you. When you sit on your bike with the pedal in the lowest position, you should be able to rest your heel on the pedal.

After checking the size of your bike, check to see that it has the right safety equipment. Your bike should have everything shown below.

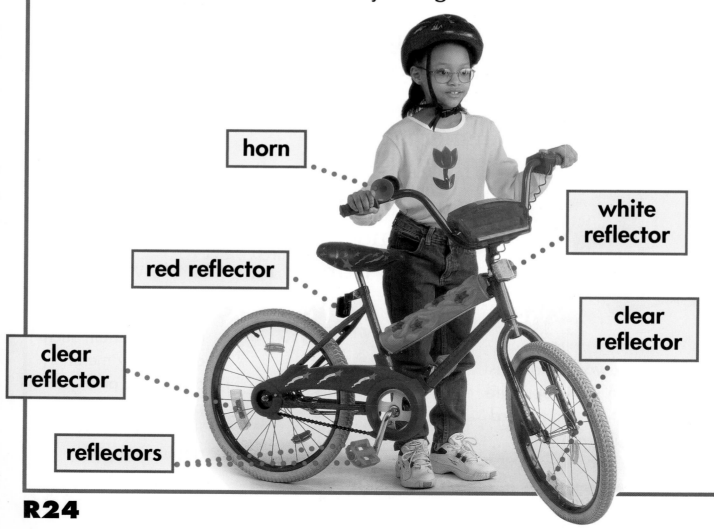

horn

white reflector

red reflector

clear reflector

clear reflector

reflectors

Your Bike Helmet

◄ Always wear a bike helmet. Wear your helmet flat on your head. Be sure it is strapped tightly. If your helmet gets bumped in a fall, replace it right away, even if it doesn't look damaged.

Safety on the Road

- Check your bike for safety every time you ride it.
- Ride in single file. Ride in the same direction as traffic.
- Stop, look, listen, and think when you enter a street or cross a driveway.
- Walk your bike across an intersection.
- Obey all traffic signs and signals.
- Don't ride at night without an adult. Wear light-colored clothing and use lights and reflectors for night riding.

Visit the Multimedia Science Glossary to see pictures of these words and to hear the words pronounced: **www.harcourtschool.com/science**

A

air

What people breathe but can not see, taste, or smell. It is a natural resource. (C29)

attract

To pull something. (F33)

algae

Plantlike living things found in water. (B40)

C

change

To make different. (E25)

amphibian

An animal with smooth, wet skin. (A52)

condense

To change from water vapor into tiny drops of water. (D18)

curve

To bend along a path. (F10)

enrich

To make better. (B12)

desert

A dry place. (B31)

evaporate

To change from water into water vapor. (D18)

dissolve

To mix a solid with a liquid completely. (E17)

extinct

Kinds of plants or animals that are no longer living. (C14)

R27

F

fall

The season that follows summer. (D43)

fossil

Parts and imprints of a plant or an animal that lived long ago. (C9)

float

To stay on top of a liquid. (E13)

force

A push or a pull. (F5)

flowers

The parts of a plant that make seeds. (A27)

forest

A place where many trees grow. (B27)

fresh water

Water that is not salty. It is a natural resource. (C33)

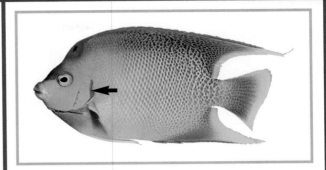

gills

Body parts that help a fish take air from water. (A47)

friction

A force that makes it harder to move things. (F20)

H

hatch

To break out of an egg. (A60)

G

gas

Matter that does not have a shape of its own, such as air. (E21)

I

insect

An animal that has three body parts and six legs. (A55)

R29

lake

A body of water with land all around it. (C34)

liquid

Matter that flows to take the shape of its container. (E9)

larva

A caterpillar. (A66)

living

Needing food, water, and air to live and grow. (A11)

leaves

The plant part that makes food for the plant. (A26)

M

magnet

A piece of iron that pulls things made of iron. (F33)

magnetic force

The pulling force of a magnet. (F43)

matter

Everything around you. (E5)

magnetize

To give magnetic force to something a magnet attracts. (F47)

mineral

One kind of nonliving thing that is found in nature. (C27)

mammal

An animal that has hair or fur and feeds its young milk. (A50)

moon

The brightest object in the sky at night. (D28)

motion

Movement from one place to another. (F13)

 nonliving

Not needing food, water, and air and not growing. (A11)

musical instrument

Something used to make music. (E47)

 ocean

A large, deep body of salt water. (B39)

 natural resource

Something found in nature that people can use. (C23)

pitch

How high or low a sound is. (E44)

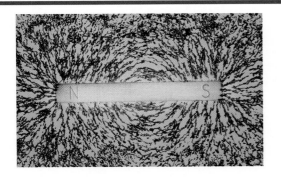

poles

The places where the pulling force of a magnet is strongest. (F39)

pull

To tug something closer. (F5)

pollen

The powder in flowers that helps flowers make seeds. (B13)

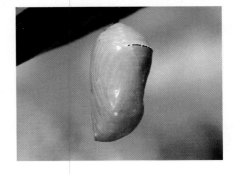

pupa

A hard covering over a caterpillar. (A67)

product

Something that people make from other things. (B16)

push

To press something away. (F5)

R

rain forest

A forest that is wet all year. (B35)

repel

To push away. (F40)

recycle

To collect things so they can be made into new things. (C40)

reptile

An animal with rough, dry skin. (A52)

reduce

To use less of a natural resource. (C38)

reuse

To use things again. (C39)

river

A body of moving water that is larger than a stream. (C34)

rotates

Spins like a top. (D32)

rock

A hard, nonliving thing that comes from Earth. (C5)

S

sand

Tiny, broken pieces of rock. (C6)

roots

Plant parts that hold plants in the soil and take in water. (A24)

season

One of four times of the year—fall, winter, spring, and summer. (D35)

R35

seed

What most plants grow from. (A29)

shelter

A place where an animal can be safe. (B8)

seed coat

Covering a seed may have. (A29)

sink

To drop to the bottom of a liquid. (E13)

senses

Touch, sight, smell, hearing, and taste. (A5)

solid

Matter that keeps its shape. (E6)

sound

Everything you hear. (E35)

stars

Objects in the sky that give off light. (D28)

speed

How quickly or slowly something moves. (F15)

stem

Plant part that helps hold up the plant and moves water to the leaves. (A25)

spring

The season that follows winter. (D35)

stream

A body of moving water smaller than a river. (C34)

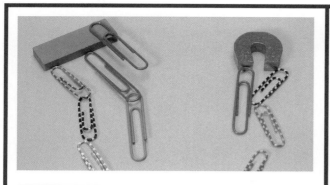

strength

How strong something is, such as a magnet's pull. (F37)

sunlight

Light from the sun. (A34)

summer

The season that follows spring. (D39)

surface

The top or outside of something. (F19)

sun

The closest star to Earth. (D28)

tadpoles

Young frogs that hatch from eggs. (A72)

temperature

The measure of how hot or cold something is. (D9)

water cycle

The movement of water from Earth to the sky and back again. (D18)

thermometer

A tool that measures temperature. (D9)

water vapor

Water that you can not see in the air. (D18)

vibrate

To move back and forth very fast. (E36)

weather

What the air outside is like. (D5)

R39

wheel

A roller that turns on an axle. (F23)

wind

Moving air. (D13)

winter

The season that follows fall. (D47)

A

B

S

Sand, C6
  in a liquid, E17
Science skill
  classify, A48, B14,
    B38, C4, E4, F8
  communicate, A32,
    B34, C36, D26
  compare, A10, A22,
    A58, B26, C12,
    D4, E8
  draw a conclusion,
    B30, C32, E20,
    F22, F46
  estimate, E29
  form a hypothesis,
    E16, E46
  gather data, C22,
    E12, F32
  graph, D51, E7
  infer, C28, D16, D34,
    F38
  investigate, B10, D46,
    E24, E34, F4, F42
  make a model, A54,
    C8, D30
  measure, D8, E40,
    F18
  observe, A4, A28,
    A42, A64, B4, D12
  order, D38
  predict, D42, F12
  sequence, A70
  use numbers, E8, E40
Seasons, D24–D25,
    D34–D50
  fall, D42–D45
  spring, D34–D37
  summer, D38–D41
  winter, D46–D49

Seeds
  carried by animals,
    B10–B12
  in fall, D44
  growth of, A29
  inside of, A28
  planting, D36
  seed coat of, A29
  sprouting, D34
  types of, A30–A31
  and Water,
    experiment, A1
Senses, A2, A4–A9
Shade in the forest,
    B27
Shape
  changing, E25–E26
  of gases, E21
  of liquids, E9
  of solids, E6
  of solids that sink or
    float, E12–E14
Shelter
  in forest, B29
  for people, B15–B16
  plants as, B8–B9
Ships, E29
Sight, A5–A6
Sink, E12–E15
Sky, D26–D28
Sleet, D19
Smell, A5, A9
**Snacks, making
    trail mix,** B20
Snow, D19, D47
Soil, C25
  enriched by animals,
    B11–B12
  in a forest, B27
  in a liquid, E17
  as a resource, C25

Solids, E4–E7
  changing, E25
  in a liquid, E1,
    E16–E17
Solutions, E18–E19
Sounds, E33–E48
  changing loudness of,
    E38
  made by musical
    instruments,
    E47–E48, E50
  made by vibrations,
    E36–E37, E48–E49
**South pole (of
    magnet),** F40–F41
S pole, F40–F41
Speed, F15
Spring, D25,
    D34–D37
Stars, D27–D29
Staying safe,
    R22–R25
Stem, A23, A25, A29
**Stopping
    movement,** F6
Stream, C34
Strength of magnet,
    F37
Summer, D25,
    D38–D41
Sun, D28–D31
  giving heat, D11,
    D31
  giving light, A34,
    D31
  and water cycle,
    D18–D19
Sunlight
  in desert, B31
  in fall, D43–D44
  in forest, B27–B28

Photography Credits

Page Placement Key: (t) top, (c) center, (b) bottom, (l) left, (r) right, (fg) foreground, (bg) background, (i) inset

Cover: Kevin Schaffer; (bg) Norbert Wu.

Table of Contents: Pg.*4 (fg) Robert Canis/Masterfile; (bg) Andre Gallant/The Image Bank; *5 (fg) Art Wolfe; *6(fg) Bios(W.Fautre)/Peter Arnold, Inc.; *7 (fg)(t) Kevin Galvin/The Stock Market; (b) Rod Planck/Photo Researchers; (bg) Jeff Smith/The Image Bank; *8 (fg) Nesbitt Grammar/FPG International; (bg)Telegraph Color Library/FPG International; *9 (fg)Tim Young/Stone.

UNIT A: Pg. (fg) Robert Canis/Masterfile; (bg) Andre Gallant/The Image Bank; A2-A3 Ron Kimball Photography; A3 (i) Ray Mathis/A5 Picture It; A6 David Waldorf/FPG International; A8-A9 (t) DiMaggio/Kalish/The Stock Market; A8 (b), A9 (b) Laura Dwight Photography; A11 Gene Peach/Index Stock; A12 (l) John Gerlach/Animals Animals/Earth Scenes; A12 (r) Mitsuaki Iwago/Minden Pictures; A13 (l) Barry L. Runk/Grant Heilman Photography, Inc.; A13 (r) Michael Groen Photography; A14 (l) Victoria Hurst/Tom Stack & Associates; A14 (r) Laura Dwight/Peter Arnold, Inc.; A15 (l) Werner H. Muller/Peter Arnold, Inc.; A15 (r) Jeff Foott/Bruce Coleman, Inc.; A17 Stephen Ogilvy/Picture It; A18 (tl) Tony Freeman/PhotoEdit; A18 (tlc) Michael Groen Photography; A18 (tc) Sonya Jacobs/The Stock Market; A18 (trc) George Mattei/Envision; A18 (tr) John Fowler/Valan Photos; A18 (brc) A. Ramage/Animals/Animals/Earth Scenes; A19 Michael Groen Photography; A20-A21 Frans Lanting/Minden Pictures; A21 (i) Richard Shiell/Animals Animals/Earth Scenes; A25 (t) Bill Bachman/Photo Researchers; A26 (tl), A26 (br) Runk/Schoenberger/Grant Heilman Photography, Inc.; A26 (tr) Greg Vaughn/Tom Stack & Associates; A26 (tr) Don Mason/The Stock Market; A26 (bl) Colin Milkins/Animals Animals/Earth Scenes; A27 Rich Miller/AG Stock USA; A29 (tr) Joseph Nettis/Stock, Boston; A29 (cr) D. Cavagnaro/Visuals Unlimited; A29 (bl) Paul Barton/The Stock Market; A29 (br) Michael Groen Photography; A30 (tl) Stephen J. Krasemann/DRK Photo; A30 (l) Barry L. Runk/Grant Heilman Photography, Inc.; A30 (br) Inga Spence/Tom Stack; A30 (cr) Ed Young/AG Stock USA; A30 (tl) Gerard Lacz/Peter Arnold, Inc.; A30 (tr) Ed Young/AG Stock USA; A30-A31 Tom Bean/DRK Photo; A31 (bl) G.I. Bernard/Animals Animals/Earth Scenes; A31 (br) Runk/Schoenberger/Grant Heilman Photography, Inc.; A31 (cl) Barry L. Runk/Grant Heilman Photography, Inc.; A31 (cr) Runk/Schoenberger/Grant Heilman Photography, Inc.; A31 (tr) D. Trask/The Stock Market; A33 Glenn Oakley/AG Stock USA; A35 (l) Larry Ulrich/Tony Stone Images; A35 (r) Bill Brooks/Masterfile; A36 (t) National Gallery London/Superstock; A38 (a) Superstock; A38 (b) Jerry Howard/Positive Images; A38 (c) Tim McKenna/The Stock Market; A38 (d) Lynwood M. Chase/Photo Researchers; A38 (e) T. A. Wiewandt/DRK Photo; A38 (f) D. Cavagnaro/Visuals Unlimited; A38 (top-all), A38 (g), A39 (b) Runk/Schoenberger/Grant Heilman Photography, Inc.; A39 (t) Fred Bruemmer/DRK Photo; A40-A41 Kim Taylor/Bruce Coleman, Inc.; A41 (tl) J. C. Carton/Bruce Coleman, Inc.; A41 (tr) Hans Reinhard/Bruce Coleman, Inc.; A41 (bl) Michael Fogden/DRK Photo; A43 S. Nielsen/DRK Photo; A44 (tl) Dick Canby/DRK Photo; A44 (tr) Steve Bly/Tony Stone Images; A44 (bl) Tom Tietz/Tony Stone Images; A44 (br) Hans Reinhard/Bruce Coleman, Inc.; A45 (t) Belinda Wright/DRK Photo; A45 (b) Frans Lanting/Minden Pictures; A46 (t) Merlin Tuttle/Photo Researchers; A46 (c) Ralph Ginzburg/Peter Arnold, Inc.; A46 (b) Melissa Cummings/Georgia DNR, Wildlife Resources Division, Public Affairs Office; A47 (l) Ken Howard/The Wildlife Collection; A47 (c) G. I. Bernard/Animals Animals/Earth Scenes; A49 (bc) Jane Burton/Bruce Coleman, Inc.; A49 (br) Joe McDonald/Tom Stack & Associates; A49 (bl) Patricia Doyle/Tony Stone Images; A49 (c) Lemoine Jacana/Photo Researchers; A51 (tr) Marian Bacon/Animals Animals/Earth Scenes; A50 (t) Stephen J. Krasemann/DRK Photo; A50 (bl) Ed Reschke/Peter Arnold, Inc.; A50 (br) M. Rutz/Natural Selection; A51 (a) Anthony Mercieca/Photo Researchers; A51 (tr) Frans Lanting/Minden Pictures; A51 (b) M. H. Sharp/Photo Researchers; A52 (t) David Muench/Tony Stone Images; A52 (c) Tui de Roy/Minden Pictures; A52 (b) Suzanne L. Collins/Photo Researchers; A53 (t) Charles V. Angelo/Photo Researchers; A53 (b) Brian Parker/Tom Stack & Associates; A55 John Mitchell/Photo Researchers; A56-A57 (b) Richard L. Carlton/Photo Researchers; A56 (t) A. Ramage/Animals Animals/Earth Scenes; A57 (t) Zefa/Brockhaus/The Stock Market; A57 (c) Robert & Linda Mitchell; A59 (t) Jane Burton/Bruce Coleman, Inc.; A59 (b), A60 (bl), A60 (br) Jane Burton/DK Photos; A60 (tl), A60 (tr), A61 (tr) Jane Burton/Bruce Coleman, Inc.; A61 (tr), A61 (bl), A61 (br) Jane Burton/DK Photos; A62 (t) Bob Bennett/The Wildlife Collection; A62 (c) Robert Winslow/Natural Selection; A62 (b) John Giustina/The Wildlife Collection; A63 Stefan Lundgren/The Wildlife Collection; A65 Mesza/Bruce Coleman, Inc.; A66 (t) Ed Reschke/Peter Arnold, Inc.; A66 (b) Michael Fogden/DRK Photo; A67 (tl) Jeff Foott/DRK Photo; A67 (tr) D. Cavagnaro/DRK Photo; A67 (b) Harry Rogers/Photo Researchers; A68-A69 (c) Gary Vestal/Tony Stone Images; A68 (t) Sturgis McKeever/Photo Researchers; A68 (r) John Fowler/Valan Photos; A69 (r) Nancy Rotenberg/Animals Animals/Earth Scenes; A71 Dalton/Animals Animals/Earth Scenes; A72-A73 Michael Groen Photography; A72 (l) Brent P. Kent/Animals Animals/Earth Scenes; A72 (r) John M. Burnley/Photo Researchers; A72 (c), A73 (l) Runk/Schoenberger/Grant Heilman Photography, Inc.; A73 (r) Joe McDonald/Animals Animals/Earth Scenes; A74 Stephen Ogilvy/Picture It; A75 (t) Kjell Sandved/Butterfly Alphabet; A75 (b) Michael Groen Photography; A76 (top row left to right) Patricia Doyle/Tony Stone Images; A76 (3) Breck P. Kent; A76 (4) David M. Dennis/Tom Stack & Associte; A76 (5) Doug Wechsler/Animals Animals/Earth Scenes; A76 (6) J. H. Robinson/Animals Animals/Earth Scenes; A76 (bottom) (a). Jeff Foott/DRK Photo; (b). A. Ramage/Animals Animals/Earth Scenes; (c). Joe McDonald/Animals Animals/Earth Scenes; (d). Runk/Schoenberger/Grant Heilman Photography, Inc.; (e). Dick Canby/DRK Photos; (f). David Muench/Tony Stone Images; (g) Michael Fogden/DRK Photo; (h) Brian Parker/Tom Stack & Associates; (i) Jane Burton/DRK Photo; A77 Gary Vestal/Tony Stone Images; A80 Richard Ellis/Sygma.

UNIT B: Pg. (fg) Art Wolfe; B2-B3 Gregory Ochocki/Photo Researcher, Inc.; B3 (l) E.F. Anderson/Visuals Unlimited; B4 (t) Roy Morsch/Stock Market; B5 Wayne Lankinen/Bruce Coleman, Inc.; B6 (l) Chris Jones/The Stock Market; B6 (r) Zefa-Brockhaus/The Stock Market; B7 (l) John Chellman/Animals Animals/Earth Scenes; B7 (r) Beth Davidow /Visuals Unlimited; B8 (t) Tom Brakefield/DRK Photos; B8 (b) Raymond A. Mendez/Animals Animals/Earth Scenes; B9 (t)Scott Nielson/Bruce Coleman, Inc.; B9 (bl) Wendell Metzen/Bruce Coleman, Inc.; B9 (br) Jeff Foot/Bruce Coleman, Inc; B12 (t)Patti Murray/Animals Animals/Earth Scenes; B12 (b) Breck P. Kent/Animals Animals /Earth Scenes; B13 Darlene A. Murawski/Peter Arnold, Inc.; B15 Richard Hutchings/Picture It; B16 (t) Jon Feingersh/The Stock Market; B16 (c) Aaron Haupt/Photo Researchers; B16 (b) Pete Saloutos/The Stock Market; B17 (t) Stephen Ogilvy/Picture It; B17 (b) Hank Morgan/Rainbow; B18 (t) Larry Lefever/Grant Heilman Photography; B18 (br) Michael Groen Photography; B20 (b) Stephen Ogilvy/Picture It; B21 (t) Eric Horan; B21 (b) Michael Groen Photography; B22 (tl) Tom Bean/DRK Photo; B22 (tl) Hans Reinhard/Bruce Coleman, Inc.; B22 (tr) Tom Bean/DRK Photo; B22 (tc) Darlyne A. Murawski; B22 (cr) Raymond A. Mendez/Animals Animals/Earth Scenes; B22 (bl) Breck P. Kent/Animals Animals/Earth Scenes; B22 (br) Michael Groen Photography; B27 Stephen J. Krasemann/DRK Photos; B28 (t) Pat OiHara/Tony Stone Images; B28 (r) James H. Robinson/Animals Animals/Earth Scenes; B29 (t) Art Wolfe/Tony Stone Images; B29 (tr) Robert Lubeck/Animals Animals/Earth Scenes; B29 (b) R.A. Simpson/Visuals Unlimited; B31 Daniel J. Coc/Natural Exposure; B32 (t) Nora & Rick Bowers/The Wildlife Collection; B32 (bl) M.P. Kahl/DRK Photo; B32 (br) Jeff Foott/DRK Photos; B33 (t) Leonard Lee Rue III/Bruce Coleman, Inc.; B33 (c) Runk Schoenberger/Grant Heilman Photography, Inc.; B33 (b) Joe McDonald/Animals Animals/Earth Scenes; B35 Michael Sewell/Peter Arnold, Inc.; B36 (l) Michael Fogden/DRK Photo; B36 (r) Ed Wheeler/The Stock Market; B37 (t) Softlight Photography/Animals Animals/Earth Scenes; B37 (b) David Matherly/Visuals Unlimited; B39 David Hall/Photo Researchers; B40-B41 Doug Perrine/DRK Photo; B40 (l) Doug Perrine/Innerspace Visions; B41 (tr) Fred Winner/Jacana/Photo Researcher; B41 (br) Dave B. Fleetham/Visuals Unlimited; B42 (tl) Sullivan & Rogers/Bruce Coleman, Inc.; B42 (tc) Edgar T. Jones/Bruce Coleman, Inc.; B42 (tr) Patti MurrY/Animals Animals/Earth Scenes; B43 (t) Tom & Therisa Stack/Tom Stack & Associates; B44 (tl) Stephen J. Krasemann/DRK Photo; B44 (tlc)Doug Perrine/DRK Photo; B44 (trc) Nora & Rick Bowers/The Wildlife Collection; B44 (tr) Ed Wheeler/The Stock Market; B44 (cl) Stephen J. Krasemann/DRK Photo; B44 (cc) John Kaprielian/Photo Researchers; B44 (cr) Randy Morse/Tom Stack & Associates; B44 (b) Michael Seward/Peter Arnold, Inc.; B44 (b) Daniel J. Cox/Natural Exposures; B48 Meldren W. Anderson.

UNIT C: Pg. (fg) Bios (W. Fautre)/Peter Arnold, Inc.; C2-3 Neil Alexander/Black Star; C3 (i) D.Cavagnaro/DRK Photo; C5 Jeremy Woodhouse/DRK Photo; C6 Michael Groen Photography; C7 (l)Ted Horowitz/The Stock Market; C7 (r)Myrleen Ferguson/Photo Edit; C9 Pascal Goetgheluck/Science Photo Library/Photo Researchers; C10-11 The Natural History Museum, London; C10 (t) J & L Webber/Peter Arnold, Inc.; C10 (b) Dr. Paul A. Zahl/Photo Researchers; C11 (t) D.L. Dilcher/Florida Museum of Natural History; C11 (b) Ted Clutter/Photo Researchers; C11(b) E.R. Degginger/Bruce Coleman, Inc.; C14 (t) Alex Kerstitch/Bruce Coleman,Inc.; C14(cl) E.R. Degginger/Color- Pic; C14 (cr) R. Mariscal/Bruce Coleman, Inc.; C14 (bl) Martin Land/Science Photo Library/Photo Researchers; C14 (br) Ed Reschke/Peter Arnold, Inc.; C15 (l) Jonathan Blair/Woodfin Camp & Associates; C15 (r) Frans Lanting/Minden Pictures; C16 (t) Rock painting of a leaping cow and frieze of small horses, 15000BC, Caves of Lascaux, Dordogne, France/Bridgemand Art Library; C18 (tl) Alex Kerstitch/Bruce Coleman, Inc.; C18 (tr) Frans Lanting/Minden Pictures;

C18 (a.) J&Lwebber/Peter Arnold, Inc.; C18 (b.) Paul E. Jones/Gamma Liaison International; C18 (c.)Larry Ulrich/DRK Photo; C18 (d.) Jonathan Blair/Woodfin Camp&Associates; C23 Georgia Dept. of Natural Resources; C24 (l) Virginia P. Weinland/Photo Researchers; C24 (r) Old Hickory Furniture Co.; C25 Mark E. Gibson; C25 (t) E.R. Degginger/Color- Pic; C26 (t) J-C Carton/Bruce Coleman, Inc.; C26 (cl) Joyce Photo/Photo Researchers; C26 (cr) Tino Hammid/Gemological Institute of America; C27 (tl) Dr. E.R. Degginger/Color-Pic; C29 Myrleen Ferguson/Photo Edit; C30 (l)Gary Withey/Bruce Coleman, Inc.; C30 (r) Tom Stack/Tom Stack & Associates; C31 (l) Michael Groen Photography; C31 (r)Runk Schoenberger/Grant Heilman Photography, Inc.; C33 Bob Daemmrich Photography; C34 (bl) Michael P. Gadomski/Photo Researchers; C34 (br) Matt Bradley/Tom Stack & Associates; C34 (t) Michael De Young/Uniphoto; C35 (bl)Julie Houck/Uniphoto; C44 (a.) Julie Houck/Uniphoto; C44 (b.) Michael DeYoung/Uniphoto; C44 (c.)Matt Bradley/Tom Stack & Associates; C44 (e.) Joyce Photo/Photo Researchers; C44 (f.)Myrleenson/Photo Edit; C48 State of Indiana Department of Natural Resources.

UNIT D: Pg. (fg)(t) Kevin Galvin/The Stock Market; (b) Rod Planck/Photo Researchers; (bg) Jeff Smith/The Image Bank; D2-3 Keith Kent/Science Source/Photo Researchers; D3 (i) Carl Wolinsky/Stock, Boston; D5 Stephen Ogilvy/Picture It; D5 (bg) Robert Brenner/Photo Edit; D6 (bl) Michael Newman MR/Photo Edit; D6 (br) Richard Price/FPG International; D6 (tl) J & M Studios/Gamma-Liaison International; D6 (tr) Timothy Shonnard/Tony Stone Images; D7 (t)Rudi Von Briel/Photo Edit; D7 (b)Weather Services International; D9 Dale Spartas/Gamma-Liaison International; D9 (b) Michael Groen Photography; D10 (bl)(tr) Michael Groen Photography; D10 (c) Stephen Ogilvy/Picture It; D10 (tl) Joe Sohm/Image Works; D11 Richard Hutchings/Picture It; D13 (t) Michael Groen Photography; D13 Terje Rakke/ Image Bank; D14 (insets) Michael Groen Photography; D14-15 Gene Peach/Gamma-Liaison International; D15 (t)Everett Johnson/Frozen Images; D17 Joe McDonald/Visuals Unlimited; D17 (bkgd) Michael Dwyer/Stock Boston; D20 Richard Hutchings/Picture It; D21 The Granger Collection, NY; D22 (2) Bob Daemmrich/Stock Boston; D22 (3) Jim Scourletis/Index Stock Photograph, Inc.; D22 (4) Michael Groen Photography; D24-25 Tom Bean/DRK Photo; D25 (l) Robert Ginn/Photo Edit; D25 (r) Barbara Cushman Rowell/DRK Photo; D27 (bg) H.Armstrong Roberts, Inc.; D28 (l) Dale Boyer/Photo Researchers; D28 (t) (stars) Roger Ressmeyer/Corbis; D28 (r) Lester Lefkowitz/The Stock Market; D29 (t) Dan Suzio/Photo Researchers; D29 (r) NASA/Mark Marten/Photo Researchers; D29 (c) Rev. Ronald Royer/Science Photo Library/Photo Researchers; D29 (b) US Geological Survey/Science Photo Library/Photo Researchers; D31 M. Timothy OiKeefe/Bruce Coleman, Inc.; D32 (i) Mark Phillips/Superstock; D33 (b) H. Armstrong Roberts, Inc.; D35 Mark Reinstein/Uniphoto; D35 (l)Jan Halaska/Photo Researchers; D36 (t) Ping Amranand/Uniphoto; D36 (c) Uniphoto; D36 (b) E. Webber/Visuals Unlimited; D37 (tl) Gregory K. Scott/Photo Researchers; D37 (br) Sonda Dawes/Image Works; D37 (b) Jane Burton/Bruce Coleman, Inc.; D39 D.Young Wolff/Masterfile; D39 (i) Jan Halaska/Photo Researchers; D40 (l) J.C. Carton/Bruce Coleman, Inc.; D40 (c) Gay Bumgarner/Tony Stone Images; D40 (r) Nigel Cattlin/Photo Researchers; D41 (t) Tom Brakefield/Bruce Coleman, Inc.; D41 (b) M.P. Kahl/DRK Photo; D43 Paul Barton/The Stock Market; D43 (i) Jan Halaska/Photo Researchers; D44-45 (t) Henry R. Fox/Animals Animals/Earth Scenes; D44 (tl)Frank Siteman/Stock,Boston; D44 (bl) Alan L. Detrick/Photo Researchers; D44 (br) Laura Riley/Photo Researchers; D45 (l) William J. Weber/Visuals Unlimited; D47 Bill Horsman/Stock Boston; D47 (i) Jan Halaska/Photo Researchers; D48 (t) W. A. Banaszewski/Visuals Unlimited; D48 (b) L. West/Photo Researchers; D49 (l) Karl & Steve Maslowski/Photo Researchers; D49 (r) N. Benvie/Animals Animals/Earth Scenes; D50 (tl), (tr), (c) Photograph by Ansel Adams, (c)1998 by the Trustees of the Ansel Adams Publishing Rights Trust. All Rights Reserved; D53 (t) Michael Groen Photography; D56 The Franklin Institute Science Museum/Peter Olson.

UNIT E: Pg. (fg) Nesbit Grammar/FPG International; (bg) Telegraph Colour Library/FPG International; E2-E3 D. Cavagnaro/DRK Photo; E3 (i) Michael Fogden/Animals Animals/Earth Scenes; E10 Michael Groen Photography; E14-15 Michael Groen Photography; E22 (t) Stephen Ogilvy/Picture It; E23 (t)Michael Groen Photography; E25 Stephen Ogilvy/Picture It; E26 (b) Stephen Ogilvy/Picture It; E26 (t) & E27 Michael Groen Photography; E28 (b) Michael Groen Photography; E28 (t) Beatrice Hatala/RMN/Musee Picasso, Paris; E29 (t) Tony Freeman/Photo Edit; E30 (2) Stephen Ogilvy/Picture It; E30 (3) Joseph Nettis/Stock, Boston; E30 (4) Michael Groen Photography; E30 (5) Stephen Ogilby/ Picture It; E30 (6) Kathy Tarantola/Index Stock photography, Inc.; E30 (tc) Stephen Ogilvy/Picture It; E30 (tl) Michael Groen Photography; E31 Michael Groen Photography; E32-33 Luray Caverns,VA; E35 From the 131st Edition of the Ringling Brothers, Barnum and Bailey Circus. Ringling Brothers, Barnum and Bailey Circus and the Greatest Show on Earth are registered trademarks; E38 (t)Steve/Bourgeois/ Unicorn Stock Photos; E39 (t)Kunio Owaki/The Stock Market; E39 (b) Gayna Hoffman/Stock, E41Jeff Greenburg/Unicorn Stock Photos; E41 (i)John Elk III/Bruce Coleman, Inc.; E42-43 (i)Gordon R. Gainer/The Stock Market; E42 (cr)David Muench; E42 (r)Reed Williams/Animals Animals/Earth Scenes; E42 (b) Lynn M. Stone/Index Stock Photography; E44 (tl) Richard/Megna/Fundamental Photographs; E44 (tr) Walter Chandoha; E47 Bob Daemmrich/Stock,Boston; E49 (r)Florent Flipper/Unicorn Stock Photos; E52 (3.) Steve Bourgeois/Unicorn Stock Photos; E56 Georgia Rural Telephone Museum.

UNIT F: Pg. (fg) Tim Young/Stone; F2-3 D. Cavagnaro/DRK Photo; F3 (i) Michael Fogden/Animals Animals/Earth Scenes; F5 Michael Groen Photography; F6 (t) Shellie Nelson/Unicorn Stock Photos; F7 Stephen Ogilvy/Picture It; F9 Jeff Greenburg/Unicorn Stock Photos; F10 (t) John MacPherson/The Stock Market; F10 -11 (b) Addison Geary/Stock ,Boston; F11 (c.) Michael Groen Photography; F11 (tr) Ed Harp/Unicorn Stock Photos; F13 Michael Groen Photography; F14-15 Richard Hutchings /Picture It; F16-17 (t) Stephen Ogilvy/Picture It; F17 (t) Kimberly Burnham/Unicorn Stock Photos; F20 Richard Hutchings/Picture It; F21 Michael Groen Photography; F23 Chuck Savage/The Stock Market; F24 (r) Jeff Greenberg/Visuals Unlimited; F24 (tr) Michael Groen Photography; F25 (t) Leslye Borden/Photo Edit; F25 (b) Stephen Ogilvy/Picture It; F26 (r) Eric Bouvet/Gamma Liaison International; F28 (a.) John MacPherson/The Stock Market; F28 (c.) Chuck Savage/The Stock Market; F28 (d.) Shellie Nelson/Unicorn Stock Photos; F28 (e.) Richard Hutchings/Picture It; F30-31 Papolla/Photo Edit; F33 Michael Groen Photography; F34 Peter Cade/Tony Stone Images; F34 (i) Michael Groen Photography; F35 (tr) Breck P. Kent/Animals Animals/Earth Scenes; F36-37 Michael Groen Photography; F40 Stephen Ogilvy/Picture It; F41 Richard/Megna/Fundamental Photographs; F43 Stephen Ogilvy/Picture It; F47 Arthur R. Hill/Visuals Unlimited; F48 Stephen Ogilvy/Picture It; F49 Sal Dimarco/Black Star/Harcourt; F51 (t) Adrienne Hart-Davis/ Photo Researchers, Inc.; F53 (tl) Michael Groen Photography; F53 (t) Richard Megna/Fundamental Photographs; F53 (b) Kiribati/The Stock Market; F56Courtesy of Brookhaven National Laboratory.

Glossary: Pg. R26 (t) Gary Withey/Bruce Coleman, Inc.; R26 (cl) Randy Morse/Tom Stack & Associates; R26 (bl) Doug Wicksler/Animals Animals/Earth Scenes; R27 (tl) John MacPherson/The Stock Market; R27 (tr) Breck P. Kent/Animals Animals/Earth Scenes; R27 (cl)Daniel J. Cox /Natural Exposures; R27 (br) Alex Kerstitch/Bruce Coleman, Inc.; R28 (tl)Paul Barton/The Stock Market; R28 (tr)Pascal Goetgheluck/Science Photo Library/Photo Researchers; R28 (cl) Joseph Nettis/Stock, Boston; R28 (c)Michael Groen Photography; R28 (b)Stephen J.Krasemann/DRK Photo; R28 (t) ClaudeGuillaumin/Tony Stone Images; R29 (tr) Brian Parker/Tom Stack & Associates; R29 (cr)Jane Burton/DK Photos; R29 (b)Michael Groen Photography; R30 (tl)Matt Bradley/Tom Stack & Associates; R30 (cl)Michael Fogden/DRK Photo; R31 (cr)Dr. E.R. Degginger/Color-Pic; R31 (bl)Patricia Doyle/Tony Stone Images; R31 (b)Dale E. Boyer/Photo Researchers; R31 (br) Roger Ressmeyer/Corbis; R32 (tl)Addison Geary/Stock, Boston; R32 (tr)Michael Groen Photography; R32 (c) Bob Daemmrich/Stock, Boston; R32 (r)John Kaprielian/Photo Researchers; R32 (bl) Georgia Dept. of Natural Resources; R32 (br)Ron Kimball Photography; R33 (t) Richard Megna/Fundamental Photographs; R33 (tr)Shellie Nelson/Unicorn Stock Photos; R33 (c)Darlyne A. Murawski/Peter Arnold, Inc.; R33 (cr)Jeff Foot/DRK Photo, R33 (br)Ed Harp/Unicorn Stock Photos; R34 (tl)Michael Sewell/Peter Arnold, Inc.; R34 (tr) Stephen Ogilvy; Picture It; R34 (cr) David Muench/Tony Stone Images; R35 (tl)Michael P.Gadomski/Photo Researchers; R35 (c) Michael Groen Photography; R35 (bl)Lynwood M.Chase/Photo Researchers; R35 (br) Jan Halaska/Photo Researchers; R36 (tl)Runk/Schoenberger/Grant HeilmanPhotography; R36 (r)Art Wolfe/Tony Stone Images; R36 (cl)T.A. Wiewandt/DRK Photo; R36 (bl)Stephen Ogilvy/Picture It; R37 (tl)From the 131st Edition of the Ringling Brothers, Barnum and Bailey Circus and The Greatest Show on Earth are registered trademarks; R37 (tr) Roger Ressmeyer/Corbis; R37 (cl)Richard Hutchings/Picture It; R37 (cr)Superstock; R37 (bl) Mark Reinstein/Uniphoto; R37 (br)Michael Deyoung/Uniphoto; R38 (cl)D. Young Wolff/Photo Edit; R38 (cr) Richard Hutchings/Picture It; R38 (bl)Lester Lefkowitz/The Stock Market; R38 (br) Runk Schoenberger/Grant Heilman Photography; R39 (tl) (cl)Michael Groen Photography; R39 (br)Bob Daemmrich/Stock, Boston; R40 (t) Richard Hutchings/Picture It; R40 (c)TerjeRakke/The Image Bank; R40 (b) Bill Horsman/Stock,Boston.

All other photographs by Harcourt School Publishers, © Harcourt.

Illustration Credits

Michael Mayduk B11, C10, C13; Tim Haggerty C17; Corbert Gauthier D18-19; Christer Eriksson D32, D33; Margarita Cruz E14-15; Rachel Geswaldo (electronic art) F16-17.